THE DAY
GOD
RESTED

philip arnold

CLAY BRIDGES
PRESS

The Day GOD Rested

Copyright © 2023 by Philip Arnold
Published by Clay Bridges Press in Houston, TX
www.claybridgespress.com

Unless otherwise indicated, scripture quotations are taken from the ESV® Bible (The Holy Bible, English Standard Version®), copyright © 2001 by Crossway, a publishing ministry of Good News Publishers. Used by permission. All rights reserved.

Scripture quotations marked (NKJV) are taken from the New King James Version®. Copyright © 1982 by Thomas Nelson. Used by permission. All rights reserved.

Scripture quotations marked (NASB) are taken from the (NASB®) New American Standard Bible®, Copyright © 1960, 1971, 1977, 1995, 2020 by The Lockman Foundation. Used by permission. All rights reserved. www.lockman.org

ISBN: 978-1-68488-053-9 Paperback
ISNB: 978-1-68488-075-1 Hardback
eISBN: 978-1-68488-054-6

Special Sales: Clay Bridges Press titles are available in special quantity discounts. Custom imprinting or excerpting can also be done to fit special needs. Contact Lucid Books at Info@claybridgespress.com

Table of Contents

How to Read This Book

The Sabbath is the seventh Day of the week which THE LORD has set aside for HIS People as a Holy Day of rest. This book is written for the purpose of better understanding what GOD has said about HIS Holy Day in HIS WORD and what that means for us today.

The Sabbath is not only The Day of rest, but the word *Sabbath* actually means "rest" or more literally "to stop or cease." It can also mean "to sit, to dwell, or to remain." The word *Sabbath* in English is very similar to its original pronunciation in its original language of Hebrew. The original word looks like this שבת and is pronounced "Shabbat." It's easy to see the similarity between the English "Sabbath" and the Hebrew "Shabbat," and they both mean exactly the same thing: the seventh day. For this reason, you will see these words used interchangeably throughout this book.

You will also notice throughout this book that some words are printed in blue and some in red. The reason for this is simple. There is a theme of blue running throughout SCRIPTURE in association with GOD'S WORD, and I always liked the way JESUS'S WORDS are printed in red in THE GOSPELS. So anywhere in this book where SCRIPTURE is quoted, it will be printed in blue, and any SCRIPTURE quotes in this book where THE LORD is speaking directly will be printed in red.

I want to be clear in this next statement. Neither this book or its author belong to or is influenced by any particular denomination. And just because this is a book about The Sabbath does not automatically mean that I share any of the doctrinal beliefs of any particular denomination. I have to say this so that it will be known to the reader that this book is based solely on SCRIPTURE and linguistics. I did the very best I could to leave my own opinion out of it as much as possible.

In writing this book, the idea was to take the most exhaustive SCRIPTURAL study of The Sabbath and condense it down into the smallest and easiest to digest kind of study guide possible for the reader's sake. That being said, it is made up of 12 chapters and 42 BIBLE studies that make up those chapters. Each chapter is titled after its own theme, which is relevant to The Sabbath. And each chapter contains several BIBLE studies, each one further explaining a different aspect of the chapter's title theme.

Each BIBLE study contains several BIBLE verse quotes, which you will find at the beginning of each BIBLE study; these are meant to be read and studied before and during the actual study. Here is another statement I want to make very clear. This book is not meant to be read without the use of a BIBLE. **_Do not_** read these BIBLE studies without referencing, reading, and understanding the verses quoted in each study. If you do, you will miss so much of the meaning contained in those studies. In fact, many of the studies are written in such a way that if you don't read and understand the verse quotes, you will not understand most of that particular study.

Now that all that's out of the way, how much does THE BIBLE actually say about The Sabbath? Well . . .

שבת
Ha Shabbat / The Sabbath

Genesis 1:1-31

Genesis 2:1-3

Exodus 1:8-14

Exodus 5:4-19

Exodus 6:5-9

Exodus 12:14-16

Exodus 14-16

Exodus 16:4-30

Exodus 18:13-23

Exodus 20:8-11

Exodus 23:9-12

Exodus 31:12-17

Exodus 33:12-14

Exodus 34:21

Exodus 35:1-3

Leviticus 6:12-13

Leviticus 16:29-31

Leviticus 19:1-4

Leviticus 19:9-10

Leviticus 19:30

Leviticus 23:1-3

Leviticus 23:22

Leviticus 23:26-32

Leviticus 24:1-9

Leviticus 25:1-55

Leviticus 26:1-2

Leviticus 26:12-13

Leviticus 26:27-43

Numbers 15:30-36

Numbers 28:1-10

Deuteronomy 5:12-15

Deuteronomy 6:4-9

Deuteronomy 8:2-3

Deuteronomy 11:11-12

Deuteronomy 11:18-20

Deuteronomy 15:1-5

Deuteronomy 15:12-15

Deuteronomy 23:24-25

Deuteronomy 24:17-22

1 Kings 5:3-5

2 Kings 4:18-23

2 Kings 11:1-12:15

2 Kings 16:17-18

1 Chronicles 9:32

1 Chronicles 28:1-7

2 Chronicles 22:10-24:14

2 Chronicles 36:20-21

Nehemiah 1:1-3

Nehemiah 9:13-14

Nehemiah 10:28-31

Nehemiah 13:15-22

Psalm 51:15-17

Psalm 92:1-15

Psalm 127:1-2

Proverbs 18:1

Proverbs 23:4-5

Isaiah 1:11-17

Isaiah 28:11-13

Isaiah 46:9-10

Isaiah 55:1-3

Isaiah 56:1-8

Isaiah 58:6-14

Isaiah 60:1-18

Isaiah 61:1-3

Isaiah 66:15-23

Jeremiah 17:19-27

Jeremiah 25:8-14

Lamentations 2:5-6

Ezekiel 2:9-3:3

Ezekiel 20:10-26

Ezekiel 22:6-16

Ezekiel 22:26-31

Ezekiel 23:38-39

Ezekiel 44:23-24

Ezekiel 45:13-17

Ezekiel 46:1-5

Daniel 7:23-25

Hosea 2:8-11

Amos 8:1-10

Matthew 4:1-4

Matthew 5:17-19

Matthew 6:8

Matthew 6:24-34

Matthew 7:12

Matthew 11:27-12:14

Matthew 13:22

Matthew 24:15-21

Matthew 27:57-28:7

Mark 1:21-31

Mark 2:23-3:6

Mark 6:1-2

Mark 6:30-32

Mark 12:28-34

Mark 15:42-16:6

Luke 4:1-4

Luke 4:14-22

Luke 4:31-39

Luke 6:1-11

Luke 7:18-23

Luke 8:14

Luke 10:38-42

Luke 13:10-17

Luke 14:1-24

Luke 23:50-24:6

John 1:1-4

John 1:29

John 4:5-34

John 5:5-18

John 6:22-68

John 7:14-24

John 9:1-16

John 10:7-11

John 19:30-20:23

Acts 1:12

Acts 13:13-48

Acts 15:21

Acts 16:13

Acts 17:2-4

Acts 18:4-5

Acts 20:7-12

Romans 12:1-2

Romans 14:5-6

1 Corinthians 15:45-47

1 Corinthians 16:1-4

2 Corinthians 3:16-18

Galatians 5:1

Colossians 2:13-17

Hebrews 3:7-4:11

Hebrews 10:19-25

1 John 4:19

Revelation 1:10

Revelation 10:1-11

Revelation 19:11-16

Revelation 20:4-6

Revelation 21:22-25

Revelation 22:3-5

Yep that's a lot of verses. These are all the passages that make up the 42 BIBLE studies I mentioned earlier. But for the sake of studying and learning about only The Sabbath, you might be relieved to know that not every one of these passages is directly relevant to The Sabbath. Many of them were added to different studies throughout the book because they really help to explain the subject matter of the particular studies they were added to. So, for those of you who only want a list of the verses that directly mention The Sabbath, a shorter list of verses has also been included.

Direct Mention Verses

Genesis 2:1-3

Exodus 16:4-30

Exodus 20:8-11

Exodus 23:9-12

Exodus 31:12-17

Exodus 34:21

Exodus 35:1-3

Leviticus 16:29-31

Leviticus 19:1-4

Leviticus 19:30

Leviticus 23:1-3

Leviticus 23:26-32

Leviticus 24:1-9

Leviticus 25:1-55

Leviticus 26:1-2

Leviticus 26:27-43

Numbers 15:30-36

Numbers 28:1-10

Deuteronomy 5:12-15

2 Kings 4:18-23

2 Kings 11:1-12:15

2 Kings 16:17-18

1 Chronicles 9:32

2 Chronicles 22:10-24:14

2 Chronicles 36:20-21

Nehemiah 9:13-14

Nehemiah 10:28-31

Nehemiah 13:15-22

Psalm 92:1-15

Isaiah 1:11-17

Isaiah 56:1-8

Isaiah 58:6-14

Isaiah 66:15-23

Jeremiah 17:19-27

Lamentations 2:5-6

Ezekiel 20:10-26

Ezekiel 22:6-16

Ezekiel 22:26-31

Ezekiel 23:38-39

Ezekiel 44:23-24

Ezekiel 45:13-17

Ezekiel 46:1-5

Hosea 2:8-11

Amos 8:1-10

Matthew 11:27-12:14

Matthew 24:15-21

Matthew 27:57-28:7

Mark 1:21-31

Mark 2:23-3:6

Mark 6:1-2

Mark 15:42-16:6

Luke 4:14-22

Luke 4:31-39

Luke 6:1-11

Luke 13:10-17

Luke 14:1-24

Luke 23:50-24:6

John 5:5-18

John 7:14-24

John 9:1-16

John 19:30-20:23

Acts 1:12

Acts 13:13-48

Acts 15:21

Acts 16:13

Acts 17:2-4

Acts 18:4-5

Colossians 2:13-17

Hebrews 3:7-4:11

Shabbat Is a Gift from GOD

Genesis 2:1-3

THE LORD rested on Shabbat.
HE Blessed and Sanctified Shabbat.

Exodus 16:4-30

Emphasis on verse 29.
THE LORD has given you The Sabbath.

Exodus 20:8-11

THE LORD rested on Shabbat.

Exodus 31:12-17

THE LORD rested and was refreshed.

Lamentations 2:5-6

THE LORD takes away a blessing, not a curse.

Hosea 2:8-11

THE LORD takes away a blessing, not a curse.

Mark 2:23-3:6

Emphasis on verse 27.
The Sabbath was made for Man.

Introduction to Chapter 1
From GOD and Not from Man

It is a sad fact that most Churches today would consider The Sabbath as something legalistic, almost like a burdensome ritual they might be forced to observe. Because of views like these, it is necessary to highlight the fact that Shabbat or . . . The Sabbath, is a good gift from GOD. It was not initiated or instituted by Man. It was all GOD'S idea and thank HIM for it.

Genesis 2:1-3
Exodus 20:8-11
Exodus 31:12-17

1.1 The Day GOD Rested

In these verses we read that THE LORD HIMSELF rested on Shabbat. Exodus 31:16-17 even says, "HE rested and was refreshed." Did HE get tired and need a break? Absolutely not. THE LORD is ALMIGHTY; HE never slumbers or sleeps. HE is completely self-sufficient, self-energizing, and self-sustaining; HE would absolutely never "need" a break like we do. So, why did HE rest, and why was HE refreshed?

When attempting to answer this question, it is important to first point out the fact that the word for "rested" in the above SCRIPTURE quote in the original Hebrew is the word שבת or Sabbath. And as mentioned in the Preface, this word doesn't only mean rest. It can also mean "to cease." So this verse could just as accurately be translated, "HE ceased and was refreshed." I think this possible translation is an important consideration when attempting to answer the initial question because it's fairly easy to see just how drastically it would change the meaning of this verse in English.

However, I do have a slightly more speculative answer. Have you ever done something not because of a need but purely for the enjoyment or appreciation of it? For example, if my wife makes my favorite meal and sets it out on the kitchen counter, I'm probably going to take at least a bite of it even if I'm not hungry, just because I like the taste. Even if I don't have an immediate need to have food in my stomach, I will still taste it just to savor the flavor. I believe that is what it was like for THE ALMIGHTY when HE rested and was refreshed on Shabbat. HE didn't need to rest. I think HE simply wanted a moment to sit back, observe, and admire the beautiful Creation HE had made, take a sigh of relief, and say it is "very good." And so HE would have been "refreshed" by the relief that HIS Creation was finished.

1. Why do you think GOD rested on the seventh day?

_____

_____

_____

2. Was there ever a time in your life when you were relieved because you finally finished a really big project?

_____

_____

_____

3. Does the memory of that time affect the way you see and understand THE LORD'S completion of Creation?

_____

_____

_____

Additional Notes:

_____

_____

_____

_____

_____

_____

_____

Genesis 2:1-3
Exodus 16:4-30
Lamentations 2:5-6
Hosea 2:8-11
Mark 2:23-3:6

1.2 A Holy Gift

Speculations aside, HE did rest on Shabbat. And we can also read in Genesis 2:1-3 that THE LORD Blessed and Sanctified Shabbat specifically because it's The Day that HE rested from HIS work in Creation. And that's The Day HE gave to us so that we could rest as well. What a magnificent honor and privilege that HE would give us such a day. How could we possibly be as appreciative and grateful as we ought to be for such a Holy gift?

It is absolutely mind-boggling to think that over the centuries, this Holy Day has come to be thought of by some as legalistic or a burdensome ritual. In Lamentations 2:5-6 and Hosea 2:8-11, the context is clear that GOD is punishing and disciplining HIS People. Both of these passages also make mention of THE LORD taking Shabbat away from HIS People as a means of punishment. So was HE punishing them by taking something legalistic and burdensome away from them? That wouldn't make much sense, would it? If a Parent is going to punish their child, they don't do it by telling them that they are no longer allowed to do the chore they hate the most. That would be no punishment at all, would it? But what would they do as punishment? Wouldn't they take away the toy that the child loves the most—something the child will actually miss and grieve over not having it? So it is with The Sabbath in these two passages. It was taken away as a punishment because it was considered to be a Day that is Holy, special, and cherished as well it should be.

YESHUA said it best in Mark 2:27: "The Sabbath was made for Man, not Man for The Sabbath." Man was not made for The Sabbath to observe it legalistically as some kind of weekly ritual. Of course, it is also not legalistic to keep Shabbat in the manner that THE LORD instructed us to in HIS WORD. But The Sabbath was made as a day of rest for Man in the very beginning because GOD knew we would need it. And the message is basically the same in Exodus 16:29 when HE says, "See! THE LORD has given You The Sabbath." The people of Israel at that time were refusing to take advantage of and even spurning what GOD had given them by continuing to work on Shabbat despite the instruction of GOD. May we all show more love and gratitude than that for The Goodness GOD has shown to us.

1. Why do you think so many people consider Shabbat to be
    a burden or legalistic? What could have caused such an
    opinion?

    _____

    _____

    _____

2. After reading these verses, do you think of Shabbat as a "have
    to" or a "get to"?

    _____

    _____

    _____

3. Was there ever a time in your life when THE LORD was
    trying to do something good for you, but you weren't willing
    to receive it?

    _____

    _____

    _____

Additional Notes:

    _____

    _____

    _____

    _____

    _____

    _____

CHAPTER 2

The Necessity of Shabbat

Exodus 1:8-14
Why we need Shabbat.

Exodus 5:4-19
Why we need Shabbat.

Exodus 18:13-23
Why we need Shabbat.

Exodus 20:8-11
Shabbat is Blessed and Sanctified.
Give rest to others.

Exodus 23:9-12
A Sabbath for The Land.
Give rest to others.

Leviticus 25:1-55
A Sabbath for The Land.

Leviticus 26:27-43
A Sabbath for The Land.

Deuteronomy 5:12-15
Remember that you were a slave and
therefore give rest to others.

Deuteronomy 11:11-12
A Land that THE LORD cares for.

2 Chronicles 36:20-21
The Land had rest for 70 years.

Psalm 127:1-2
Why we need Shabbat.

Isaiah 28:11-13
Give rest to the weary.

Jeremiah 25:8-14
The Land had rest for 70 years.

Mark 6:30-32
Why we need Shabbat.

Introduction to Chapter 2
THE LORD Knows What HE's Doing

Have you ever heard people say things like this: "I'll rest when I'm dead?" Such a mentality is common and even encouraged in the world today. But it is THE LORD who is THE CREATOR of everything including the human mind and body. And because HE is THE CREATOR of every human mind and body, HE knows exactly what they need in order to be strong, happy, and healthy. Namely, rest. This flies in the face of what most people want to do—especially workaholics. But it is GOD HIMSELF who has told us to take a day of rest. In this chapter, we will be discussing why HE did that.

Exodus 1:8-14
Exodus 5:4-19
Exodus 18:13-23
Psalm 127:1-2
Mark 6:30-32

2.1 Shabbat Is for the Weary

Can you remember a time when you were extremely overworked to the point of exhaustion? I would be willing to bet that just about everyone reading this could probably remember some such a time whether it was for a day, a week, a month, a year, or even several years. And depending on the intensity of the workload and the length of time it is continued, this can become a very destructive lifestyle.

It could be something you are being afflicted with by someone else as in Exodus 1:8-14 and Exodus 5:4-19. Or it could be something that is simply required of you by the situation at hand as in Mark 6:30-32. Or maybe it is something you are actually doing to yourself out of a lack of good judgment as in Exodus 18:13-23 and Psalm 127:1-2. All these are exactly the type of situations that Shabbat is meant to be a relief from.

THE LORD does want you to have a good work ethic. HE also wants you to demonstrate it to others so that you represent HIM well and so that you may accomplish the work HE has given you to do. This concept is especially obvious after reading only a few chapters in Proverbs. But HE does not want you to work so hard for so many hours that it begins to take a toll on your physical and mental health.

1. Was there ever a time in your life when you were extremely overworked to the point of exhaustion?

_____

_____

_____

2. Was it done to you by someone, or did you do it to yourself?

_____

_____

_____

3. How does that make you think about THE LORD'S Sabbath?

_____

_____

_____

Additional Notes:

_____

_____

_____

_____

_____

_____

Exodus 20:8-11
Exodus 23:9-12
Deuteronomy 5:12-15
Isaiah 28:11-13

2.2 Give Rest to the Weary

The People of Israel were brought out from under the oppressive slavery of pharaoh and the egyptians by THE MIGHTY HAND OF GOD and given rest in place of their chains. HalleluYAH to The GOD of freedom (Deuteronomy 5:12-15)! And because they had been in slavery, they were in the position to be the most appreciative and grateful for the rest that they had been given.

They were instructed to remember what they were freed from and how THE LORD freed them. And that this memory of their own liberation was to be their motivation to take that gift of rest and pay it forward by giving it to others. And yet we know from Isaiah 28:12 and from history that they eventually began to neglect that gift.

Whether you have ever been a slave or not, we can all do what we can to pay it forward as well. Because The Day is not given only to great, wealthy, influential, or famous people. But we read in Exodus 20:8-10 and Exodus 23:12 that foreigners, servants, and even cattle were also to be given rest on Shabbat. What can you do to give rest to those around you?

1. What kind of bondage has GOD freed you from?

_____

_____

_____

2. Is there anything in your life that you have enslaved yourself to?

_____

_____

_____

3. What can you do to give rest to those around you?

_____

_____

_____

Additional Notes:

_____

_____

_____

_____

_____

_____

Exodus 23:9-12
Leviticus 25:1-55
Leviticus 26:27-43
Deuteronomy 11:11-12
2 Chronicles 36:20-21
Jeremiah 25:8-14

2.3 That the Land May Enjoy Its Sabbaths

In both Exodus 23:10-11 and Leviticus 25:1-7, THE LORD tells
HIS People that The Land itself is to have a Sabbath and that
every **seventh** year is to be a whole year of rest for The Land. In
Leviticus 26:27-43, HE tells them what kind of future Judgments
and Punishments HE will give them if they don't obey HIM
when they are living in HIS Land. One of the Punishments HE
promises them in verses 33-35 and 43 is that HE would "scatter
them among the nations" and that while they were there, The
Land would "lie desolate" and "enjoy its Sabbaths." THE LORD
was telling them in advance what the Punishment would be
because HE already knew that they would disobey HIM.

And later on we can see this verified in the book of Jeremiah. In
Jeremiah 25:8-14 THE LORD is speaking through The Prophet
to The People and telling them that HE is about to bring that
very Punishment on them just like HE said HE would back in
Leviticus 26:33-35 and 43. THE LORD says in Jeremiah 25:11-
12 that the "whole land shall become a ruin and a waste" while
The People "serve the king of babylon seventy years." And 2
Chronicles 36:20-21 not only confirms how this Punishment
happened to Israel, but also quotes both passages of SCRIPTURE
from Jeremiah and Leviticus when it says, "until The Land had
enjoyed its Sabbaths" and "to fulfill seventy years."

But why exactly does The Land need a Sabbath in the first place?
Here we have another BIBLICAL Instruction that has been long
since verified and proven necessary by modern science. The
fact of the matter is that not only The Land of Israel but any
land that is used for farming or growing crops may have its soil

depleted of minerals if it is used constantly and without rest. And after doing this for a certain span of time, it will result either in a lack of crops altogether or in a nutrient deficiency in the foods grown on that soil. And such a deficiency would inevitably cause a lack of nutrition for The People living on that soil.

Deuteronomy 11:11-12 says that The Land of Israel is "a land that THE LORD Your GOD cares for" and that "THE EYES of THE LORD are always upon it." Because of passages like this, it would be easy to assume that GOD is giving a Sabbath to The Land purely for The Land's sake. And in one sense that is true because HE does care for The Land. But that is not the main reason why HE gave a Sabbath year to The Land. HE tells us the reason in the first two passages we discussed at the beginning of this study. In both Exodus 23:10-11 and Leviticus 25:1-7, THE LORD tells them to let The Land rest and not to reap or sow anything so that when The Land produces of itself, there will be food for everyone. That's the reason for The Sabbath rest year for The Land. In summary, we can safely say that The Sabbath Day is established so that everyone can rest, and The Sabbath year for The Land is established so that everyone can eat. Allowing The Land to have that year to rest will ensure that the soil will be replenished for the next seven years.

1. Can you think of any other reasons why the land should also be given a Sabbath rest?

_____

_____

_____

2. What are some other ways that people could benefit by giving the land its Sabbath rests?

_____

_____

_____

3. How do these concepts apply to people receiving their rest?

_____

_____

_____

Additional Notes:

_____

_____

_____

_____

_____

_____

_____

Our GOD Is Merciful and Kind

Exodus 1:8-14
What the enemy wants to do.

Exodus 5:4-19
What the enemy wants to do.

Exodus 6:5-9
THE LORD brought HIS People out from under their burdens.

Exodus 14-16
What did GOD do for Israel as soon as they came out of Egypt?

Exodus 33:12-14
Emphasis on verse 14. THE LORD will give you rest.

Leviticus 26:12-13
THE LORD has broken the bars of slavery.

Isaiah 28:11-13
Give rest to the weary.

Daniel 7:23-25
What the enemy wants to do.

Matthew 11:27-12:14
Come to THE LORD and HE will give you rest for your souls.

Mark 6:30-32
Come away and rest a while.

Galatians 5:1
YESHUA set us free.

Introduction to Chapter 3
GOD Is Good

Yes, GOD is Good. This is probably the most well-known and most repeated saying in all of Christianity, but it is still very true. It was also true when GOD gave us The Sabbath. Shabbat itself is a very good gift from GOD to us. Here's the problem. Just about everyone has a different idea of what is good, but that doesn't trip HIM up. If anyone ever misunderstands GOD'S Goodness, HE has already given us an amazingly accurate representation of HIS Goodness in HIS WORD. And if anyone wanted to find out exactly what kind of Good GOD is, all they would have to do is read THE BIBLE. The purpose of this chapter is to contrast the nature and desires of GOD to the nature and desires of the enemy and to see the character and kindness of our GOD that made HIM want to give us The Sabbath in the first place. From this, we will have much to Glorify GOD for.

Exodus 1:8-14
Exodus 5:4-19
Daniel 7:23-25

3.1 Overbearing Oppression

We know the enemy comes to steal, kill, and destroy. But how does he do this? Most of the time, he is subtle and creeping and will not announce what he intends to do to you in an obvious way. It is not unusual throughout history for the enemy to directly influence an oppressive regime in order to persecute GOD'S People. It is the fourth beast in Daniel 7:23-25 who seeks to wear out the Saints of THE MOST HIGH. This is the character of the enemy and is exactly what we see happening in Exodus 1:8-14 and Exodus 5:4-19. That is who the enemy is, and that is his personality. It is his natural desire to want to oppress, enslave, overburden, and wear out GOD'S People. But our GOD is not like that. Our GOD is the exact opposite.

1.   What are some of the ways the enemy tries to oppress you or take away your peace?

_____

_____

_____

2.   What do you think GOD'S solution is for that situation?

_____

_____

_____

3.   How much time have you spent in Prayer about that situation?

_____

_____

_____

Additional Notes:

_____

_____

_____

_____

_____

_____

_____

Exodus 6:5-9
Exodus 14-16
Exodus 33:12-14
Leviticus 26:12-13
Isaiah 28:11-13
Matthew 11:27-12:14
Mark 6:30-32
Galatians 5:1

3.2 Breaking the Yoke

All these verses encourage and reassure us by reminding us of what kind of GOD we serve. How Great is HIS Mercy and Compassion and Loving Kindness toward HIS People! It is HIS HEART to give rest and relief to those who are oppressed and heavily burdened—whether that burden is from actual physical labor or from other circumstances and trials in life. On The Sabbath THE LORD HIMSELF rested and was refreshed, and HE wants to give you that same rest. THE LORD'S desire is to give you rest and peace because HE is such a Good FATHER. Always remember that.

Every one of these passages show us the character and The Kindness of Our GOD. But I want to draw your attention especially to Exodus 14-16. Yes, we are going to cover three whole chapters in this study. But don't worry. We will be covering them in a way that is quick and easy. A brief summary of these three chapters of SCRIPTURE could be this.

Exodus 14	THE LORD brings Israel through The Reed Sea (also known as the Red Sea) and drowns the egyptians.
Exodus 15:1-21	Israel gives Glory to GOD for their Salvation from Egypt.
Exodus 15:22-27	THE LORD gives them water.
Exodus 16	THE LORD gives them manna and The Sabbath.

What is the purpose for this breakdown of these three chapters? It shows you exactly what GOD did as soon as The People crossed The Reed Sea. The first things HE did for them was to bring them to springs of water; then HE gave them The Manna and The Sabbath. In other words, the very first thing HE did for them immediately after they came out of slavery was to give them water, food, and rest. That is the kind of GOD we serve. Praise HIS GREAT NAME for HE is Good and Kind to all who call on HIM!

1. What do you think it was like for the Israelites to see The Goodness and Provision of GOD compared to their slavery in Egypt?

    _____

    _____

    _____

2. What comes to your mind when you think of The Goodness of GOD? Have you ever asked HIM for a greater revelation of HIS Goodness?

    _____

    _____

    _____

3. Have you ever witnessed The Goodness of GOD or the Supernatural Provision of GOD in your life? If so, how did it change you?

    _____

    _____

    _____

Additional Notes:

_____

_____

_____

_____

_____

_____

_____

CHAPTER 4

The Day Is Holy

Genesis 1:1-31
No sign for Shabbat.

Genesis 2:1-3
Set apart "from" all the other days in Creation.

Exodus 16:4-30
Holy "to" THE LORD.

Exodus 20:8-11
Remember Shabbat to keep it Holy.

Exodus 31:12-17
Holy "for" You. Holy "to" THE LORD.

Exodus 35:1-3
Holy "to" THE LORD.

Leviticus 23:1-3
A Sabbath "to" THE LORD. HIS Day.

Leviticus 24:1-9
Things that only happen on The Sabbath.

Numbers 28:1-10
Things that only happen on The Sabbath.

Deuteronomy 5:12-15
A Sabbath "to" THE LORD. Remember you were a slave.

2 Kings 16:17-18
Things that only happen on The Sabbath.

1 Chronicles 9:32
Things that only happen on The Sabbath.

Nehemiah 9:13-14
HIS Holy Day.

Nehemiah 13:15-22
You cannot profane what is common.
It must first be considered Holy.

Isaiah 56:1-8
You cannot profane what is common.
It must first be considered Holy.

Isaiah 58:6-14
HIS Holy Day.

Jeremiah 17:19-27
Set apart "from" your regular work schedule.

Ezekiel 20:10-26
You cannot profane what is common.
It must first be considered Holy.

Ezekiel 22:6-16
You cannot profane what is common.
It must first be considered Holy.

Ezekiel 23:38-39
You cannot profane what is common.
It must first be considered Holy.

Ezekiel 44:23-24
HIS Holy Day.

Ezekiel 45:13-17
Things that only happen on The Sabbath.

Ezekiel 46:1-5
Things that only happen on The Sabbath.

Introduction to Chapter 4
How Is a Day Kept Holy?

In all these SCRIPTURES, we can find THE LORD instructing us in one way or another to keep the Sabbath Day Holy. But what exactly does it mean to say that a day is Holy? Most Churches today hold to a somewhat generic definition of the word "Holy." That is "to be set apart." There is much more to it than that, and I highly recommend that you research the word throughout the rest of SCRIPTURE, but that definition is basically correct. So if a day is to be considered Holy, then there are a few questions we should ask ourselves: What is it "set apart" from? What is it "set apart" to? For what purpose is it "set apart?" And how do we as GOD'S People ensure that this day continues to be kept as "set apart?" These are the questions we will attempt to answer in this chapter.

Exodus 20:8-11
Deuteronomy 5:12-15

4.1 Remember The Sabbath because It Is Holy

How do you think about The Sabbath? Do you like so many consider it to be just an old and crusty tradition that is only for The Jews in The Old Testament to keep? Just like everything else in this life, what you do and say about Shabbat starts in the heart. You cannot think one way and act another and still be genuine. The same is true for keeping Shabbat Holy. When you sincerely want to keep Shabbat Holy, it will result in a desire to do the things that THE LORD Commands concerning HIS Sabbath. So, the first thing we have to figure out is how to keep Shabbat Holy in our hearts. If we can do that first, our actions will follow. So, how do we do it?

There is one key word that appears in both of these SCRIPTURE passages that can help us understand how to do that: Remember. In Exodus 20:8 we are instructed to "Remember the Sabbath day, to keep it holy." And in Deuteronomy 5:15, we are instructed to "remember that you were a slave in the land of Egypt" so that we will appreciate this Holy Day we have been given. Isn't it all the other days of the week that are so easily forgotten? There aren't many reasons to remember a day that is a regular, nothing out of the ordinary day. But Shabbat is the day that GOD HIMSELF has "set apart" as a day for us to rest and to meet with HIM. It is not like other days, so we should not forget or disregard it. It should be important to us because HE is important to us. And we would honor THE LORD by "remembering" and highly esteeming the day HE has made Holy. And so we would keep Shabbat Holy in our hearts.

1. When it comes to doing anything for THE LORD, is it better to do it begrudgingly or with thankfulness? Explain your answer.

_____

_____

_____

2. How do you think about The Sabbath?

_____

_____

_____

3. Where did that way of thinking come from?

_____

_____

_____

Additional Notes:

_____

_____

_____

_____

_____

_____

_____

Nehemiah 13:15-22
Isaiah 56:1-8
Ezekiel 20:10-26
Ezekiel 22:6-16
Ezekiel 23:38-39

4.2 Don't Profane The Sabbath

All these verses show that Shabbat is something that can be profaned. That might seem like an obvious statement, but it bears repeating because the difference between what is Holy and what is profane is not something that is often taught in Churches anymore. You cannot profane what is already profane, and the very fact that Shabbat can be profaned indicates its Holiness. A slightly more inclusive definition of "Holy" could be "consecrated and dedicated to THE LORD'S ways, purposes, and instructions."

Even when you are dealing with things and times that are not BIBLICALLY prescribed, if they are used or abused in ways that they were not originally intended to be used, they would be rendered in a state that anyone could recognize as "profaned." I think a few examples are in order.

Imagine that you are attending the funeral of a family member you loved very much. You are remembering them, mourning, and grieving, and there is a friend of the family who is also attending the funeral. However, instead of mourning, he is socializing, advertising his services, handing out business cards, telling jokes, and overall being very disruptive. You would be right to say that he is "profaning the time" that was "set apart" for the purpose of cherishing the memory of the one who died by using that time for purposes that it wasn't meant for and being completely insensitive to the real purpose for which the time was intended.

Now, imagine any man or woman who saw fit to wear their wedding clothes to work. If they came home from a long day's work with their wedding clothes dirty and stained, do you think for a second that their spouse would be happy with them? No. Why not? Because they used the clothing that was "set apart" for the occasion they memorialize as work clothes and treated them as if they were no different than rags to work in. At that point it would not be surprising for the spouse to say they had "profaned" their wedding clothes.

These illustrations can give us a small idea of how THE LORD must feel when HIS People violate HIS Sabbath. And if these examples of profaning everyday occurrences left a bad taste in your mouth, then how much more cautious should we be to never profane The Day that is made Holy by and for THE LORD OF GLORY!

1. Have you ever had something you considered to be special ruined by something else?

_____

_____

_____

2. What was your reaction to that, and why?

_____

_____

_____

3. Can you relate that particular incident to what THE LORD says about HIS Sabbath?

_____

_____

_____

Additional Notes:

_____

_____

_____

_____

_____

_____

_____

Genesis 1:1-31
Genesis 2:1-3
Leviticus 24:1-9
Numbers 28:1-10
2 Kings 16:17-18
1 Chronicles 9:32
Jeremiah 17:19-27
Ezekiel 45:13-17
Ezekiel 46:1-5

4.3 Set Apart from the Rest of the Week

What makes Shabbat so special? And what is it set apart "from"? In Genesis 2:1-3 we read that THE LORD Blessed and Sanctified the seventh day specifically because it is the day HE rested "from" all HIS work in Creation. HE didn't Bless and Sanctify any of the other six days of Creation. By Blessing and Sanctifying only Shabbat, HE made a distinction between it and the other days and made Shabbat set apart "from" the other six days. It is also important to note that this is the very first place in all of SCRIPTURE where the word *Holy* is used. So the very first time the word *Holy* is used, it is referring to The Sabbath. Let's take a look at some of the distinctions THE LORD made between the other days of the week and HIS Holy Sabbath.

In both Leviticus 24:1-9 and 1 Chronicles 9:32, we can see that Shabbat is The Day when The Bread of THE PRESENCE was arranged on The Table of Showbread. In Numbers 28:1-10 we can see that The Grain Offering made on Shabbat is twice as much flour as what is offered on the other days of the week. In 2 Kings 16:18 there is even a special walkway for only The King to use and only on Shabbat. And in Ezekiel 45:13-17 and Ezekiel 46:1-5, not only is there a special meal to be prepared as an offering to THE LORD on The Sabbath, but this is the only day of the week when the Gate of The Inner Court in THE TEMPLE will be opened.

Shabbat is also the only time that we have no way to verify or keep track of. What I mean by that is this. It is very clear from Genesis 1:14-18 that THE LORD gave the sun, moon, and stars so that mankind could keep track of time. And so it is. We can identify the end of a season when the sun or moon begin to come up earlier or later. We can identify the end of a month by the cycle of the moon. And we can identify the end of a day by the regular daily cycles of the sun and moon. But there is no such sign for the end of a week. If somehow everyone at the same time forgot what season, month, or day it was, they would only have to refer to the signs GOD gave in The Beginning. But the only way we can keep track of Shabbat is the fact that GOD HIMSELF has Spoken it and fixed The Time in its place. That means we all depend heavily on The Grace of GOD to be able to keep Shabbat in the first place.

And by choosing Shabbat as HIS Day of rest, HE made it set apart "from" anything related to the work that would occur throughout the rest of the week. HE ceased from HIS Work on Shabbat and, therefore, so do we. To continue to work on Shabbat would be to treat it as if it were no different from the rest of the week and therefore, it would not be kept Holy. Jeremiah 17:19-27 is one of many portions of SCRIPTURE that verify this concept. Verses 22-24 in particular draw a very clear contrast between working on Shabbat and keeping Shabbat Holy. And why? Because The People were misusing and abusing Shabbat for purposes which it wasn't intended and showing disregard for the Gift from GOD in the process.

1. There is a running theme throughout the SCRIPTURE passages that are cited in the second paragraph. Do you know what it is?

_____

_____

_____

2. Do you think that theme has any relevance to how we should keep Shabbat in modern times?

_____

_____

_____

3. What are some other ways that you could set The Sabbath apart from the rest of your week?

_____

_____

_____

Additional Notes:

_____

_____

_____

_____

_____

_____

_____

Genesis 2:1-3
Exodus 16:4-30
Exodus 31:12-17
Exodus 35:1-3
Leviticus 23:1-3
Deuteronomy 5:12-15
Nehemiah 9:13-14
Isaiah 58:6-14
Ezekiel 44:23-24

4.4 The Day Is Holy between HIM and Us

Most of these verses tell us that The Sabbath is Holy "to" THE LORD. But in Exodus 31:14, it says Shabbat is Holy "for" us. So, which one is it? Is it Holy "for" us, or is it Holy "to" THE LORD? The answer is a resounding yes. In Leviticus 23:1-2 we are given the introduction to all the Days and Times found throughout the rest of the chapter. At the end of verse 2, THE LORD calls these Days "my appointed feasts."

Of all the Times that GOD calls HIS own in this chapter, Shabbat is the very first one in verse 3. In Nehemiah 9:14, it is said in prayer and blessing to THE LORD by The Levites "your holy Sabbath." In Isaiah 58:13 THE LORD calls Shabbat "My Holy Day" and "the Holy Day of THE LORD" and in Ezekiel 44:24, HE calls them "my Sabbaths." By comparing all these verses to Genesis 2:1-3, it can be clearly seen that THE LORD set apart this Day "for" HIMSELF all the way back in Genesis. HE has given every other day to all of mankind as common days to be used for common purposes. The Sabbath is HIS day. But HE has also given this Day, which is HIS own, to us as a Day for us to rest in HIM. And so it is Holy "for" us. And we give it right back "to" HIM by putting aside the things of the rest of the week and focusing on HIM in worship and in hearing HIS WORD. And so it is Holy "to" THE LORD as well as Holy "for" us. Exodus 31:12-17 says it best when THE LORD says twice in the same passage that Shabbat is a sign forever between HIM and HIS People.

1. Who does The Sabbath belong to?

    _____

    _____

    _____

2. In your own words, what exactly would you say is so special
    about The Sabbath?

    _____

    _____

    _____

3. What are some ways that you can make your Shabbat all
    about THE LORD in order to honor HIM?

    _____

    _____

    _____

Additional Notes:

_____

_____

_____

_____

_____

_____

_____

The Colossians 2 Perspective

Until now, we have mostly discussed the goodness of The Sabbath and why THE LORD gave it to us. And so far we haven't really covered anything that was at all challenging or difficult to hear. That is about to change. At this point in the book, we will be switching gears from "the goodness of Shabbat and why GOD gave it to us" to something more like "the practical applications of how to keep Shabbat and what GOD thinks about that." Needless to say that from this point on, the teaching will be much more challenging and difficult to hear.

There is one particular Scripture passage that needs to be discussed before we go any further. That is Colossians 2:13-17 and specifically verses 16-17, which read like this:

> "16 Therefore let no one pass judgment on you in questions of food and drink, or with regard to a festival or a new moon or a Sabbath. 17 These are a shadow of the things to come, but the substance belongs to Christ."

This passage is a clear instruction that no one is to pass judgment on you for keeping or not keeping Shabbat. And it is important that we make mention of this now because as we move forward through these next chapters, you will likely feel judged. Just remember that based on this verse, no man is to judge you based on whether or not you keep The Sabbath.

Now here's the other side of the coin. Based on Matthew 5:17-19 and especially verse 19, I have a responsibility to teach not just part of THE WORD but the whole WORD. I don't want to "be called least in THE KINGDOM OF HEAVEN," so I can't just tell you the part that's easy to hear and not the part that you need to hear.

Because of that requirement, I have to tell you this: Just because keeping Shabbat does not appear to be a Salvation issue does not mean that anyone should have to be threatened with judgment or the loss of Salvation in order to obey GOD. If that is your way of thinking, then your heart is not right to begin with. GOD'S Children obey HIM out of love for HIM and a love for HIS WORD because HE has transformed their hearts, and they have a desire to obey HIM—not a desire to see how much they can get away with and still get into HEAVEN. So as we progress through these next chapters, let your love for GOD be your motivation to obey what HE has said concerning HIS Holy Day.

CHAPTER 5

A Day of Rest and No Work

Genesis 2:1-3
THE LORD ceased from HIS work on Shabbat.

Exodus 16:4-30
THE LORD knows your needs and is your Provider.

Exodus 20:8-11
Work for six days; stop work and rest the seventh day.
You and everyone who belongs to you.

Exodus 23:9-12
Work for six days; rest the seventh day.
You and everyone who belongs to you.

Exodus 31:12-17
Work for six days; stop work and rest the seventh day.

Exodus 34:21
In plowing time and in harvest, you shall rest.

Exodus 35:1-3
Work for six days; stop work and rest on the seventh day.

Leviticus 23:1-3
Work for six days; stop work and rest on the seventh day.

Leviticus 25:1-55
THE LORD knows your needs and is your Provider.

Deuteronomy 5:12-15
Work for six days; stop work and rest on the seventh.
You and everyone who belongs to you.

Psalm 127:1-2
Don't toil in vain.

Proverbs 23:4-5
Don't toil in vain.

Isaiah 28:11-13
Yet they would not hear.

Isaiah 58:6-14
Don't do what you want and still call Shabbat a delight.

Matthew 6:8
THE LORD knows your needs and is your Provider.

Matthew 6:24-34
THE LORD knows your needs and is your Provider.

Matthew 13:22
Don't let thorns get in the way.

Luke 8:14
Don't let thorns get in the way.

Luke 10:38-42
Mary had the right idea.

Luke 23:50-24:6
They rested on Shabbat according to The Commandment.

Introduction to Chapter 5
THE LORD Is Your PROVIDER

Sometimes it can be a very difficult thing to just stop working for a day, especially when you know that your income might suffer if you do. But believe it or not, GOD saw this one coming too. And while uncertain circumstances tend to make us nervous, THE LORD is a Wonderful PROVIDER. In this chapter we will be discussing exactly what that means for us in terms of priorities and dependency on HIM.

Genesis 2:1-3
Exodus 20:8-11
Exodus 23:9-12
Exodus 31:12-17
Exodus 35:1-3
Leviticus 23:1-3
Deuteronomy 5:12-15
Luke 23:50-24:6

5.1 Your Body Has to Have Rest

These verses tell us clearly that Shabbat is to be a Day of rest. As mentioned before, Genesis 2:1-3, Exodus 20:11, and Exodus 31:17 tell us that GOD HIMSELF rested on the seventh Day. And HE doesn't even need rest. HE made Shabbat a day of rest for our sake because HE knew that our physical bodies would need rest. And because HE knew we would need rest, HE made it a Commandment, not a suggestion. The women who went to YESHUA's tomb in Luke 23:54-56 knew this very well because it says in verse 56, "On The Sabbath they rested according to The Commandment."

Modern medicine and science have long since verified what GOD said in the beginning: That is that your mind and body both need a day of rest at least once a week. I would highly recommend researching what happens to your mind and body when you don't get enough sleep as well as physical rest. They will begin to deteriorate in one way or another. Your ability to think and respond quickly will become slow and dull. Your metabolism will slow way down making you overweight. And your energy level will drop dramatically making you groggy and fatigued even when you have gotten a full night's sleep. And those are just a few of the side effects. You don't need a medical degree to know that if you push yourself too much for too long a time, you will eventually burn out.

1. Are you getting enough true rest with the way your life and schedule are right now?

   _____

   _____

   _____

2. If not, what are some of the things preventing you from resting?

   _____

   _____

   _____

3. What has to happen in order for you to experience and receive the rest you need?

   _____

   _____

   _____

Additional Notes:

_____

_____

_____

_____

_____

_____

_____

Exodus 34:21
Isaiah 58:6-14
Matthew 13:22
Luke 8:14
Luke 10:38-42

5.2 Even When You Really Don't Want To

In Exodus 34:21 THE LORD tells HIS People, "In plowing time and in harvest you shall rest." Let's stop and think about the implications of that command for a moment. This command is being given directly to an agricultural society. That means the bulk of their economic success was based on what they earned from farming, growing, and harvesting their crops. The most critically important times in their economic year would have been plowing time and harvest. And so the times when they would have been the most tempted to break this command would have been plowing time and harvest. This command is the equivalent of telling a business owner not to go in to work to run his business on the day he has the potential to make the most money. What this effectively means for us (farmers and non-farmers alike) is that we must remain faithful and obedient to The Command from THE LORD even when we have every reason to want to break Shabbat.

It comes down to making a choice to keep Shabbat. Let's take a look at some SCRIPTURES that can help us make the right decision. The type of priority THE LORD wants HIS Sabbath to take in our lives can be seen plainly in Isaiah 58:13-14. Verse 13 basically says don't do what you want to do and still "call the Sabbath a delight." Both Matthew 13:22 and Luke 8:14 are recounting YESHUA'S explanation of the sower and the soil that produces thorns. In this parable, the soil is a person's heart, the seed is THE WORD OF GOD, and the thorns are the worries and cares of this world and its riches. It is easy to see how these thorns (if allowed) could grow and prevent you from keeping Shabbat—The Day which is contained within THE SEED. It is plain to see in Luke 10:38-42 that these thorns had grown around THE WORD in Martha's heart. Will you be like Martha or like Mary?

1. Can you imagine what it must have been like for the early Israelis to put their livelihood on the line for the sake of obeying THE LORD and keeping Shabbat?

   _____

   _____

   _____

2. If you were put in that exact scenario, what would you have done?

   _____

   _____

   _____

3. What are some of the things in your life that could prevent you from keeping Shabbat if you let them?

   _____

   _____

   _____

Additional Notes:

_____

_____

_____

_____

_____

_____

Exodus 16:4-30
Leviticus 25:1-55
Psalm 127:1-2
Proverbs 23:4-5
Isaiah 28:11-13
Matthew 6:8
Matthew 6:24-34

5.3 Big Blessings for Big Faith and Obedience

We read in Isaiah 28:12 that THE LORD tried to teach HIS People the concept of rest and repose, "yet they would not hear." I beg you my Brothers and Sisters, don't be like those who shut their ears to THE MOST HIGH for the sake of their own desires. Learn to die to your own desires and instead put GOD first in everything you do. Most people, young and old alike, rarely want to do what's good for them. And in this case, Shabbat is usually considered in much the same way. Both Psalm 127:1-2 and Proverbs 23:4-5 say basically the same thing: That you will waste your time working so hard for something and will even lose it before you can use it or enjoy it if THE LORD has not given it to you.

But I can assure you that GOD knows what HE'S doing when HE prescribes such a day for us. And HE has a way of making up for you more than whatever you think you would lose by not working on Shabbat. I have lost count of all the testimonies I've heard of business owners who finally made the decision to start keeping Shabbat. At first, they were nervous about losing income, but THE LORD brought them more customers and business throughout the rest of the week so that they made more money on those days than they ever could have if they had continued working on Shabbat. But if they had read, considered, Prayed about, and believed the Words of YESHUA in Matthew 6:8 and Matthew 6:24-34, they would have had no reason to fear a loss of income. And the way GOD Provided for these business owners was not a new phenomenon either. This is the way THE

LORD has always provided for HIS People. And we can see it all the way back in Exodus 16:4-5, Exodus 16:15-29, Leviticus 25:5-7, and Leviticus 25:18-22.

At first you might dread making yourself stop for a whole day. But trust me when I tell you that won't last long. It won't take very long at all for you to realize how badly you needed Shabbat all these years, and you will go from dreading it to longing for it to come at the end of the week. If you take that first leap of faith to start keeping Shabbat and stick with it, sooner rather than later, you will find yourself transitioning from saying things like, "I can't believe I don't get to do anything on Shabbat" to saying things like, "I'm so glad I don't have to do anything on Shabbat."

1. Have you ever seen THE LORD give supernatural provision in your life or in the lives of others?

    _____

    _____

    _____

2. If so, what kind of effect did it have on your Faith?

    _____

    _____

    _____

3. Do you trust GOD with your financial situation?

    _____

    _____

    _____

Additional Notes:

_____

_____

_____

_____

_____

_____

_____

CHAPTER 6

When? The Seventh Day

Genesis 1:1-31

And there was evening and there was morning.
Emphasis on verse 14.

Genesis 2:1-3

Work six days and rest on the seventh.

Exodus 16:4-30

Work six days and rest on the seventh.

Exodus 20:8-11

Work six days and rest on the seventh.

Exodus 23:9-12

Work six days and rest on the seventh.

Exodus 31:12-17

Work six days and rest on the seventh.

Exodus 34:21

Work six days and rest on the seventh.

Exodus 35:1-3

Work six days and rest on the seventh.

Leviticus 23:1-3

Work six days and rest on the seventh.
THE LORD'S appointments.

Leviticus 23:26-32

From evening to evening.

Deuteronomy 5:12-15
Work six days and rest on the seventh.

Isaiah 56:1-8
Shabbat is for everyone. Not just the Jews.

Daniel 7:23-25
Who will seek to change the times?

Matthew 27:57-28:7
Saturday is seventh. Sunday is first.
YESHUA'S Resurrection is on the first.

Mark 15:42-16:6
Saturday is seventh. Sunday is first.
YESHUA'S Resurrection is on the first.

Luke 13:10-17
Work six days and rest on the seventh day.

Luke 23:50-24:6
Saturday is seventh. Sunday is first.
YESHUA'S Resurrection is on the first.

John 19:30-20:23
Saturday is seventh. Sunday is first.
YESHUA'S Resurrection on the first.

Acts 20:7-12
Eutychus resurrected on the first day.

Romans 14:5-6
All days the same?

1 Corinthians 16:1-4
The "business" of budgeting for the collection
for The Saints on the first day.

Introduction to Chapter 6
Three Theological Positions

There are three common positions most people hold when it comes to the question of which day The Sabbath should be kept on. In this chapter we will discuss the differences between these three positions, which ones are true or false and why.

Isaiah 56:1-8
Matthew 27:57-28:7
Mark 15:42-16:6
Luke 23:50-24:6
John 19:30-20:23
Acts 20:7-12
Romans 14:5-6
1 Corinthians 16:1-4

6.1 The First and Second Opinions

The first and most common position of the three held by most Christian denominations is that The Sabbath was changed from saturday to sunday. They base this mostly on writings from "the church fathers" as well as a misapplication of a few SCRIPTURE verses.

"The church fathers" is a term used to describe those who were responsible for the formation and doctrine of the early Church during the first century and immediately afterward. In other words, the writings of the church fathers are the words of Men and not THE WORDS OF GOD. They are not SCRIPTURE and should not be relied on so heavily for any kind of doctrine as if they were.

The other part of the problem comes in when the Pastors and Teachers from these modern day denominations find certain things in The New Testament that all occur on the first day of the week (sunday). Because they then use those passages to justify the changing of The Sabbath from the seventh day (saturday) to the first day (sunday) even though the context of those passages never even suggests such a change. Let's take a look at those passages. In 1 Corinthians 16:1-4 The Apostle Paul is instructing The Church to set something aside for the collection for the Saints in Jerusalem—on the first day of the week. In Acts 20:7-12, Eutychus falls out of a window, is taken up dead, and then brought back to life—on the first day of the week. And without a doubt the most amazing of all these is found in Matthew 27:57-28:7, Mark 15:42-16:6, Luke 23:54-24:6, and John 19:30-20:2 where we read that our LORD and SAVIOR and KING was resurrected from the grave by THE FATHER—on the first day of the week.

Some of you may be thinking, "Wait a minute. You forgot about the time JESUS appeared to HIS Disciples on the first day of the week in John 20:19-23." But if you read John 19:30-20:23 in its entirety as listed at the beginning of this study, you will find two things. (1) The "first day of the week" mentioned in John 20:19 is exactly the same "first day of the week" on which YESHUA first rose from the grave, and (2) John 20:19 specifically says that HE appears to them "on the evening" that comes at the end of the "first day of the week." This means that according to the BIBLICAL reckoning of normal weekdays and depending on exactly what time of the evening it was, it may have no longer been the first day of the week by the time HE appeared to them that evening. In the BIBLICAL reckoning of days, the evening at the end of the first day would actually be considered the beginning of the second day. I realize that this may be a bit difficult to wrap your head around. If it is, then you can always skip ahead to the last study of this chapter called "When Does Shabbat Actually Start?" and then come back to this study.

These are all significant events, but none of these SCRIPTURES say anything remotely close to suggesting a change in the day that GOD chose from the seventh to the first. In fact, if you look at these same SCRIPTURES in context through a BIBLICALLY thematic lens, you find something very different.

What you find is that, generally speaking, Shabbat has a recurring theme throughout SCRIPTURE. That theme looks something like this: "Cease from your labor, don't go out of your place, rest in GOD'S PRESENCE." So if you're always resting on the seventh day, that means you're going to naturally do what on the first day? That means you're going to rise up, resume work, and be about Your FATHER'S Business on the first day. And that's exactly what we see happening with The Resurrection in THE GOSPELS. Think about it. YESHUA Resurrects on the first day (sunday morning), right? That means HE didn't Resurrect until after the seventh day was over, which also means that even in HIS death, HIS physical body still rested on Shabbat. And then immediately after Shabbat, HE rose out of that place and continued about HIS FATHER'S Business—on the first day of the week.

Most people who consider sunday to be The Sabbath also hold a belief and line of thinking that is very similar to replacement theology. That is, they think that GOD gave The Sabbath on saturday only to Israel and/or The Jewish People and that GOD does not expect the same thing from Christians or gentiles. This idea is not only lacking a BIBLICAL foundation, but it is also outright disproven by Isaiah 56:1-8.

The second position is slightly less common. That is the idea that The Sabbath can be kept on any day as long as you take a day off. You could possibly come away with this false interpretation by removing Romans 14:5-6 from the context of the rest of SCRIPTURE. But as soon as you put this passage back into the context of the rest of SCRIPTURE, you realize that Paul is not talking about whatever day of the week you choose to worship on. He is referring to The Days mentioned and explained in detail in the entire chapter of Leviticus 23. In other words, He is talking to the people who esteem one of The Appointed Times (Mo'edim) above another. For example, one person might esteem The Festival of Booths (Sukkot) above Passover (Pesakh) or if another person esteems The Day of Trumpets (Yom Teruah) above The Festival of Weeks (Shavuot). Even today, you will hear people refer to one of these Mo'edim as "The Holiest Day of the year." So it is not accurate to say that Romans 14:5-6 is referring to which day should be called The Sabbath.

The number of people who hold to this second position has unfortunately been growing. People who hold to this opinion will often say things like, "*My* Sabbath is on wednesday" or "*My* Sabbath is on monday" or whatever day they choose. They are correct when they say it is *their* Sabbath because it is their own and not GOD'S. It's the day they chose, not The Day GOD chose.

Many people will celebrate Shabbat by resting in GOD'S PRESENCE, worshiping HIM with song, praying to HIM, and reading HIS WORD. It's not at all as if Shabbat is the only day You should do those things. By all means, you should do those things as often as you possibly can. We couldn't claim to be obedient to The Greatest COMMANDMENT if it was only on one day of the week that we ever had anything to do with THE LORD. Shabbat is not the only day you should keep unto THE LORD, but it is the only day (in a regular week) that you're required to keep unto THE LORD.

1. Did you ever attend a Church or Synagogue where extra-BIBLICAL doctrine, traditions, opinions, or even false doctrine was being preached or taught?

_____

_____

_____

2. If so, how did that affect you? Did you believe it?

_____

_____

_____

3. How would you say those kinds of things could be prevented?

_____

_____

_____

Additional Notes:

_____

_____

_____

_____

_____

_____

_____

Leviticus 23:1-3
Daniel 7:23-25

6.2 Why They Are Both Wrong

Aside from the fact that most everyone who holds to these positions don't do any of the BIBLICAL requirements for The Sabbath on the day they have chosen, both of these positions have something else in common. They are both ignoring the fact that this Day is an "appointed time." THE LORD says plainly in Leviticus 23:1-3 that this Day (as well as all the other Days spoken about in Leviticus 23) is HIS "appointed time." This Day is an appointment and a time set by GOD. The question begs to be asked: Do we even have the authority or the right to change a time set by GOD? The answer is an obvious one: "No we do not." If you had any other kind of appointment, could you change the appointment time or just show up whenever you wanted? If, for example, you had a doctor's appointment for tuesday at 3:00 p.m., could you show up at 1:00 p.m. on monday and still expect the doctor to see you? If we understand that it is right to honor the times set by mere Men, how much more should we honor The Day set by GOD?

And who is it that will seek to change this time set by GOD? In Daniel 7:23-25 we read of a fourth beast, an enemy of GOD and HIS People. This beast represents a fourth kingdom, and the horns of this beast represent the kings of that kingdom. SCRIPTURE says that the eleventh horn of this beast "shall speak words against THE MOST HIGH, and shall wear out The Saints of THE MOST HIGH, and shall think to *change the times and the law*." Over the centuries, the enemy has employed many kings, emperors, commanders, officials, and all kinds of people who have power and influence to change the Times and Laws of GOD, to distort GOD'S WORD, and to oppress and persecute GOD'S People.

The Roman emperor Constantine is an example of this. He openly claimed to be a Christian and claimed that Christianity was the official religion of the Roman Empire. Yet what he actually ended up doing was creating a version of Christianity that was heavily mixed with paganism—so much so that he caused people to be more observant of the day he called "the venerable day of the *sun*" than they were of THE LORD'S Sabbath. By the way, "the venerable day of the *sun*" was a pagan holiday that was observed every "*sunday*."

Are you starting to notice the pattern yet? Is it any wonder why GOD'S People are so confused at this point when such mixed messages have been given time and time again? You need to understand that it is a recurring tactic of the enemy to use partial truths in order to perpetuate lies. So who is it that would seek to change the times set by GOD (including Shabbat) and prevent you from doing what GOD says? It is the enemy of GOD and the enemy of our souls, the devil.

1. Do you think we should Worship GOD however we choose or however HE tells us?

   _____

   _____

   _____

2. If people were to mix THE WORD OF GOD with their own preferences, what kinds of problems could that cause in society?

   _____

   _____

   _____

3. What does the fact that the enemy comes against GOD'S Appointed Times so strongly say about them?

   _____

   _____

   _____

Additional Notes:

_____

_____

_____

_____

_____

_____

_____

Genesis 2:1-3
Exodus 16:4-30
Exodus 20:8-11
Exodus 23:9-12
Exodus 31:12-17
Exodus 34:21
Exodus 35:1-3
Leviticus 23:1-3
Deuteronomy 5:12-15
Luke 13:10-17

6.3 *The BIBLICAL Sabbath*

So we've covered a lot about what there is no SCRIPTURAL evidence for. Now let's take a look at what THE BIBLE does say about when to keep The Sabbath. Every one of these SCRIPTURE passages tell us that THE LORD'S Sabbath is on the seventh day, which is saturday. We read in Luke 13:14 that even the hypocrites of YESHUA'S day knew Shabbat was on the seventh day.

Some of you may be wondering, "How do we know that saturday is the seventh day according to THE BIBLE?" This would be a fair question considering how many employers and employees alike begin their workweek on monday. It wouldn't be unreasonable for them to consider monday and not sunday as the first day of the week. But if we know that SCRIPTURE says YESHUA rose from the dead on the first day of the week and literally every denomination considers that day to be sunday, then the previous day would be the seventh or saturday. So concerning the days of the week, we have another contradiction between what THE BIBLE tells us and what the world tells us. Shocker right?

Historically speaking, The Sabbath has always been on saturday. But let's say that for some reason the vast amount of SCRIPTURAL evidence isn't enough to convince you. We also have an over-whelming amount of linguistic evidence that Shabbat is on saturday. Here is a list of translations of the word for *saturday* in 25 different languages. See if you can find any similarities.

Hebrew	Shabbat
Armenian	Shabat
Arabic	Sabet
Latin	Sabbatum
Romanian	Sambata
Greek	Savvato
Italian	Sabato
Spanish	Sabado
Portuguese	S abado
Corsican	Sabatu
Indonesian	Sabtu
Sudanese	Saptu
Somali	Sabti
Georgian	Sabati
Bulgarian	Sabota
Czech	Sobota
Polish	Sobota
Slovak	Sobota
Slovene	Sobota
Bosnian	Subota
Croatian	Subota
Serbian	Subota
Ukrainian	Subota
Russian	Subbota
Maltese	is-Sibt

1. What do you think it would be like to live in a world where everyone kept GOD'S calendar instead of their own?

_____

_____

_____

2. Do you think the similarities in pronunciation of the different words for saturday have any relevance to the weekday itself?

_____

_____

_____

3. Is there any harm in calling monday the first day of the week instead of sunday?

_____

_____

_____

Additional Notes:

_____

_____

_____

_____

_____

_____

_____

Genesis 1:1-31
Leviticus 23:26-32

6.4 When Does Shabbat Actually Start?

But deciding which day The Sabbath is on is not the only thing that needs to be straightened out here. One question most people have never asked is, "When does a day actually start?" And why would they? We have all been trained and programmed from childhood with modern methods of keeping time that a day begins at midnight. But these modern methods of keeping time are exactly that. Modern methods. How do you think people kept track of time before digital clocks, hand clocks, sundials, or even the system of 24 hours was invented? The answer is found in Genesis 1:14-18. Verse 14 in particular tells us that the sun, moon, and stars are "for signs and for seasons, and for days and years." They are the very first and most reliable clock hands mankind ever saw, and they were created by GOD HIMSELF. Using this system that GOD made, there was no 10:00 p.m., 11:00 p.m., and then midnight. There would have been no way to tell exactly when midnight was, so when did they begin a new cycle of night and day?

Our first clue is again in the very first chapter of THE BIBLE. This chapter says something very interesting every time THE LORD completes a day of Creation. It says, "and there was evening and there was morning." Nowhere in this chapter does it say, "and there was morning and there was evening." That's not in there. In every instance, it mentions evening before morning. There are also several chapters of SCRIPTURE such as Leviticus 11, 14, 15, 17, and 22 as well as Numbers 19 in which you will read the phrase "unclean until evening" over and over again. Why do you suppose it says, "until evening?" If you keep an eye out for it, you will see so many other important events and occurrences throughout SCRIPTURE that happen at evening time/sundown. That's because evening time/sundown is the BIBLICAL version of midnight. This is the time when one day ends and another begins. So according to the BIBLICAL system of days, a day actually begins on the evening of the previous day. And we can see this verified in Leviticus 23:32.

So now you have everything you need to make an informed decision about this matter straight from THE BIBLE and not based on hearsay or just what someone told you. Now, back to the original question: When is Shabbat? Answer: From friday evening to saturday evening.

1. Does the fact that a new day begins at evening time affect the way you see your daily schedule?

_____

_____

_____

2. Do you think it would have been less stressful to live in a time when you didn't have to worry about minutes or seconds?

_____

_____

_____

3. Can you think of any Prophetic implications to a day beginning at evening instead of morning?

_____

_____

_____

Additional Notes:

_____

_____

_____

_____

_____

_____

_____

CHAPTER 7

What Is Work, and What Is Not?

Exodus 12:14-16
Prepare only what you are to eat.

Exodus 16:4-30
Don't gather for yourself.
Remain in your place.

Exodus 35:1-3
Kindle no fire in all your dwelling places.

Leviticus 6:12-13
Keep the fire on the Altar burning continually.
It shall not go out.

Leviticus 19:9-10
Not work.

Leviticus 23:22
Not work.

Leviticus 24:1-9
Keep the lamps on The Menorah burning continually.

Numbers 15:30-36
Don't gather for yourself.
Don't lift a heavy load or burden.

Deuteronomy 23:24-25
Not work.

Nehemiah 10:28-31
Don't buy, sell, or do business.

Nehemiah 13:15-22
Don't work. Don't lift a heavy load or burden.
Don't buy, sell, or do business.

Isaiah 55:1-3
Come and buy without price.

Jeremiah 17:19-27
Don't work. Don't lift a heavy load or burden.

Amos 8:1-10
Don't buy, sell, or do business.

Matthew 11:27-12:14
Not work.

Mark 1:21-31
The sick were brought to YESHUA after Shabbat.

Mark 2:23-3:6
Not work.

Luke 6:1-11
Not work.

Luke 13:10-17
Shouldn't this woman be freed on The Sabbath?

Luke 14:1-24
Guiltless violation.

John 5:5-18
Guiltless violation.

John 9:1-16
Not work.

Acts 1:12
A Sabbath Day's journey.

Introduction to Chapter 7
Different Definitions

What do you call work? Is it what you do to earn a living? Or is it about physical labor? Is it about the amount of effort and energy you have to exert? Or is it a matter of doing something you really don't enjoy or what you don't want to do? All of these are reasonable answers and could accurately describe different aspects of what can be called work. In this chapter we will be exploring, not Man's common answers to these questions, but what GOD has to say about the matter from HIS WORD.

What you do for a living is considered work. I don't have any SCRIPTURE verses as a reference for this, but I think it is safe to say that anything about which you would normally say, "I'm going to work" or "I'm late for work" is to be considered work.

If anything else comes into question, your knee-jerk reaction will probably be to say something like, "That's not work to me." That would be understandable considering the fast-paced, work-oriented culture we live in today. This is the very reason why the answer to the question, "What is work?" cannot possibly be based only on what any individual does or does not enjoy doing. You might be thinking, "Well, if someone doesn't enjoy doing something, then that thing is considered work." Here's the problem with that. Plenty of people genuinely enjoy their work. Take for example people who work in professions such as a lumberjack, a contractor, a builder, or a competition weight lifter. Based on their personalities or preferences, each one of these people might honestly be able to say that they don't consider what they do to be work because they love their jobs. And yet from the outside looking in, it would be plain to see how much work is involved with such professions. So it is not an accurate gauge to say that something is only work if you don't enjoy it because then, everyone could just keep working on Shabbat simply by saying that they enjoy what they're doing.

We must remember to ask ourselves, "Am I doing what GOD wants or just what I want?" "Am I acting according to my own opinion or according to what GOD'S WORD actually says?" You will find that with enough mental effort and theological backflips, it's possible to rationalize away just about any sound doctrine. But you will also find that when one is actually looking for an answer from SCRIPTURE, it is almost always the simplest and most obvious answer that is the right one. It is almost never easy, but it is simple. So, let's take a look at some of the things that THE LORD calls working on The Sabbath in HIS WORD.

Exodus 16:4-30
Nehemiah 10:28-31
Nehemiah 13:15-22
Amos 8:1-10

7.1 Buying, Selling, and Doing Business

In Nehemiah 10:28-31 GOD'S People are rededicating themselves to HIM by taking an oath and a curse that they would walk in HIS law by keeping all HIS Commandments and Statutes and Rules. In verse 31, we can see that this includes not buying any goods or grain on Shabbat. And only a few chapters later in Nehemiah 13:15-22, Nehemiah is confronting them for breaking that oath by selling fish and all kinds of goods and foods to the people of Judah in Jerusalem on Shabbat. When confronting them in verses 17-18, Nehemiah calls it an "evil thing" and "profaning The Sabbath Day." This is the kind of language He uses to describe buying and selling on Shabbat. In Amos 8:1-10, THE LORD is chastising and passing Judgment on HIS People through The Prophet Amos. And specifically in verses 4-5, we read that one of the things HE is chastising them for is being so eager for Shabbat to be over so that they could sell grain and offer wheat for sale. This automatically indicates a much bigger problem of the attitude of their hearts toward HIS Holy Sabbath. But it also indicates that they were obviously not allowed to sell their grain and wheat on Shabbat.

So, we can see that doing business in buying and selling is one of the things that is considered working on Shabbat, not according to tradition or legalism, but according to SCRIPTURE. You may be wondering, "Why is buying and selling considered a violation of The Sabbath?" There are at least three ways to answer that question depending on whether we are talking about the buyer or the seller or both.

The first and most obvious answer is that if selling your merchandise is your main source of income, then it would be considered part of your regular job, which would be what you do for regular work.

The second answer is based on the two driving forces that keep any economy moving, which are supply and demand. By putting up your merchandise for sale on Shabbat, you are not only encouraging the buyer to come and buy your wares, but both the seller and the buyer are also creating more demand in the economy every time a transaction is made. These transactions keep the economy moving on Shabbat and encourage everyone else to keep working on Shabbat to fill that demand. So, you would actually be causing people to continue working on Shabbat.

I believe this is one of the ways GOD teaches us the concept that everything we do not only affects us, but it also affects everyone around us. And that is not only true for business; it is true for just about every aspect of this life.

The third answer is that whether you are the buyer or the seller, you are seeking your own gain and provision as opposed to relying on HIS provision. You are seeking your own increase and to further your kingdom instead of HIS KINGDOM on a Day when THE LORD alone is to be exalted. Remember this concept because it will be very important later in this chapter and in others as well. In Exodus 16:4-30 and specifically verses 5, 22, and 29, we read that THE LORD gave HIS People twice as much on the sixth day so that they would not have to gather or work for their own provision on the seventh. In a world full of people who are in one way or another set on their own greed, it's as if on Shabbat GOD is saying, "It's not about those things. Focus on ME instead of focusing on your money."

1. Can anyone really rest while the whole economy is still moving?

   _____

   _____

   _____

2. Can you think of any other ways that continuation of business on Shabbat would cause people to work on Shabbat?

   _____

   _____

   _____

3. Why do you think GOD'S People took buying and selling on Shabbat so seriously that they made an oath not to do it?

   _____

   _____

   _____

Additional Notes:

_____

_____

_____

_____

_____

_____

_____

Exodus 16:4-30
Numbers 15:30-36
Nehemiah 13:15-22
Jeremiah 17:19-27
Matthew 11:27-12:14
Mark 1:21-31
Luke 14:1-24
John 5:5-18
Acts 1:12

7.2 Physical Strain, Exertion, Manual Labor, &Travel

I think some of the most obvious things that can be called work are the things that require strength and wear out the muscles in your body. Shabbat is a Day given to THE LORD'S People for the purpose of rest. So, anything that causes strain, pain, or exhaustion really defeats the purpose of Shabbat.

In Numbers 15:32-36 we read about the man who was gathering "sticks" on Shabbat. This word for "sticks" in the Original Hebrew SCRIPTURES is the word עץ, which is pronounced *etz* and it can mean sticks, branches, wood, or trees. It is likely that this man was gathering heavy branches or even logs; he was also gathering for himself on Shabbat. This concept will be important later in this chapter.

In both Nehemiah 13:15-22 and Jeremiah 17:19-27, GOD'S People are being chastised for lifting and or carrying heaps and loads on Shabbat. The word for heaps or loads in the original Hebrew SCRIPTURES in both of these quotes is the word משא, which is pronounced *masa*. It is pretty accurately translated into English as a heap or a load. This word משא means "a burden, a load, or what is lifted and carried."

We can see from these verses that we are not to lift, bear, or carry a burden or something heavy on Shabbat. The problem is that the word **heavy** is a relative term. Exactly how heavy does a thing have to be in order to be considered a burden? There are some even today who take it to such an extreme that they won't even carry a pencil in their pocket on The Sabbath. That's a bit crazy. Even the food they ate that day adds more weight to them than that pencil does.

In John 5:5-18 YESHUA told a man HE had just healed to pick up his bed on The Sabbath and go home. Did YESHUA tell this man to sin by picking up his bed on Shabbat? Certainly not. Considering that this man was in a public place with a multitude of other invalids at the pool of bethesda, I suspect that his bed was less of a mattress and more of a cot that could be easily picked up and carried. But the question remains: How heavy does a thing have to be before it is not to be lifted on The Sabbath? There is no specific instruction in SCRIPTURE to answer this question.

One thing to remember is that you're dealing with the concept of physical rest for your physical body. There are many people who would have no problem at all lifting 10 pounds, for example. And yet there are many other people who are either elderly or suffering from other health conditions that would have a very difficult time lifting 10 pounds. You might be able to lift something really heavy (not on Shabbat) one time and not wear yourself out. But just because you are strong enough to pick up something easily doesn't mean it is not a burden. On the other hand, if you lifted something that was very lightweight one thousand times, you would definitely wear yourself out.

In either scenario, you would be putting strain on your muscles and definitely disobeying The Commandment. Here's a helpful suggestion. If a thing is not very big and bulky but you still have to use both hands to lift it, it's probably too heavy to pick up on Shabbat. And if you can't pick something up without your arms shaking under the weight of it, it's definitely too heavy to pick up on Shabbat.

In Matthew 12:4-5 YESHUA clearly indicates that there is such a thing as a "guiltless" violation of Shabbat. And in Luke 14:1-6 and particularly verse 5, YESHUA gives an example of what could be called a "guiltless violation" of Shabbat. If you ever find yourself in this type of predicament on Shabbat, the very first thing you should do is pull your Son or ox out of the well regardless of the amount of weight or what you have to do to get them out. The severity of that type of situation is the reason why it is considered a "guiltless violation."

But there are many people who when any situation whatsoever comes up on Shabbat, they will then call that situation "the ox in the ditch" and keep right on working. Have you ever done that? A situation where you simply feel compelled to continue working your regular job is not to be treated the same as or dealt with the same way as a situation where life or safety is at stake. No one has the right to say that a regular violation of Shabbat is a "guiltless violation" just because they want to keep working.

It is a good idea to take a "better safe than sorry" approach rather than use the fact that there is no specific weight limit in SCRIPTURE as a loophole to justify picking up heavier and heavier things. Trust me when I tell you that a strong desire to obey THE LORD goes a long way toward fulfilling THE LORD'S Will for your life. If you think something could be considered heavy, don't pick it up. If you think any task will become burdensome, don't do it.

In Acts 1:12 we find the phrase "Sabbath Day's journey." This phrase is used in this verse to describe the distance between the Mount of Olives where the Disciples were and Jerusalem where they were going. But you might be wondering, "What is a Sabbath Day's journey and exactly how far is it?" It is a tradition that practicing Jews came up with to prevent people from walking too far on Shabbat. Let me be clear. I am not suggesting that we should all keep this tradition. Our lives are kept and governed by THE WORDS OF GOD, by HIS Grace, and by HIS SPIRIT and not the traditions of Men.

However, you can see the reasoning for putting such a tradition in place. Because if I refrain from my regular work on Shabbat but instead I'm walking all day, I wouldn't exactly be resting, would I? So, we now have a question that is very similar to the one we discussed earlier. How far do you have to walk before it becomes work? How far do you have to walk before you begin to strain, tire, or wear yourself out? Is it the exact distance prescribed for a Sabbath Day's journey? What if you walk 10 feet more or less than the prescribed distance? What if you walk one step more or less than the prescribed distance? What if you tire yourself out before you walk a whole Sabbath Day's journey? Should you then keep walking because you haven't been required to stop by the prescribed distance? No. As you can see, drawing lines in the sand and assigning a specific distance to what a Sabbath Day's journey should be is useless. In the same way, assigning a specific weight limit to refrain from lifting on Shabbat is useless.

Let's say you weren't just stuck with walking for travel. Let's say you were driving instead. After so many hours, you would eventually get tired of driving even though it wouldn't be causing any physical strain or exertion. In fact, most travel that is any longer than a short road trip ends up being pretty tiring, which is why the first thing you want to do when you finally arrive at your destination is get some sleep. I suspect this is also the reason for the instruction we find in Exodus 16:29, which says, "remain each of you in his place" and "let no one go out of his place" on Shabbat. This Commandment is the reason why many people don't travel anywhere at all on Shabbat. It is also the reason why some people in Mark 1:32 didn't even bring their sick for YESHUA to heal them until after Shabbat was over. This is very unfortunate because if there is one day when the sick should be healed it's The Sabbath.

The fact of the matter is that anything can become work if you do it for long enough. Just make a point to not walk or travel so far or pick up something heavy or do anything that will be tiring on Shabbat because The Day is about physical rest as well as mental and spiritual rest. Make sure you stop whatever it is you're doing before you get tired from it. And again make sure you don't use this lack of a definitive stopping point as an excuse to do more than you know you should. If you start with a mentality of not wanting to keep The Commandment, you will end up breaking it. But if you have a desire in your heart to keep The Commandment and purpose yourself to put that desire into practice, you will do well.

1. How much is too much for you when it comes to lifting, walking, or traveling on Shabbat?

_____

_____

_____

2. Can you think of any problems that could be caused by assigning the same limitations or allowances to different people?

_____

_____

_____

3. Can you think of any situation in your life or someone else's that could honestly be called a "guiltless violation" of Shabbat?

_____

_____

_____

Additional Notes:

_____

_____

_____

_____

_____

_____

Exodus 12:14-16
Exodus 16:4-30
Exodus 35:1-3
Leviticus 6:12-13
Leviticus 24:1-9

7.3 Kindling Fires

In Exodus 35:3 we find The Commandment not to kindle a fire on Shabbat. There are several possible reasons for this Command. Take a moment to think about the difference between kindling a fire and just keeping a fire burning. One takes a lot more effort and *work* than the other. It only takes adding a few more pieces of wood on top of a fire in order to keep it burning. But to kindle a fire is much more of a process and a job. And even more so before the relatively newer technology of handheld lighters. First, you would have to build the fire and then you would have to use either wood friction or sparks from a flint rock to actually get a flame going. Neither one of those processes could be described as quick and easy.

Another thing to consider is how many different types of crafts and trades required the use of a fire before modern electric technology. Occupations like baking or metal working are good examples of this. These types of jobs would definitely be considered work. So without the use of a fire, many people couldn't practice their trade and therefore couldn't possibly work their regular jobs on Shabbat.

But people also had to have fires in their homes to keep warm and to cook their food. In Exodus 12:14-16, THE LORD is giving instruction concerning Passover and the first day of Unleavened Bread. This Day is also a Sabbath, and in verse 16, THE LORD says about this Day, "But what everyone needs to eat, that alone may be prepared by you." And in Exodus 16:23, THE LORD Commanded The People to set aside until morning the portion of manna that they had not yet baked or boiled. That uncooked portion of manna that was left over was what they were to eat on Shabbat; this means they had to have cooked it on Shabbat in order to eat it on Shabbat. So, how can you cook with a fire on Shabbat without kindling a fire on Shabbat? By having the fire lit and burning well before Shabbat begins. You cannot kindle what is already burning. This may be part of the reason for the Commandments in Leviticus 6:12-13 and Leviticus 24:1-4 to keep the fires on The Menorah and The Altar burning continually.

Thankfully we now live in a time when we no longer have to start a full-blown fire in order to cook our food. The modern electric technologies that occupy most kitchens today have made it so that we have that much less of an excuse to not keep this Commandment. So keep it as best as you possibly can.

1. What do you think are some other reasons for GOD giving this Command in Exodus 35:3?

    _____

    _____

    _____

2. Other than fires, can you think of anything else that would need to be prepared before Shabbat?

    _____

    _____

    _____

3. The fires on The Altar and The Menorah are never to go out and therefore would never need to be rekindled. Do you think that has anything to do with The Commandment for us to not kindle a fire on Shabbat?

    _____

    _____

    _____

Additional Notes:

_____

_____

_____

_____

_____

_____

Exodus 16:4-30
Exodus 35:1-3
Numbers 15:30-36
Nehemiah 10:28-31
Nehemiah 13:15-22
Isaiah 55:1-3
Jeremiah 17:19-27
Amos 8:1-10

7.4 A Brief Summary

Let's take a quick look at all the individual items that are indicated in SCRIPTURE as violations of The Sabbath and see whether we can find any similarities or recurring themes in them.

Exodus 16:22-30	Don't gather manna. Don't go out of Your place.
Exodus 35:3	Don't kindle a fire.
Numbers 15:32-36	Don't gather sticks.
Nehemiah 10:31	Don't buy grain or goods.
Nehemiah 13:15-22	Don't tread a wine press. Don't put heaps of food on a donkey. Don't bring heaps of food into the city. Don't sell food or other goods. Don't allow the city gates to open "for business". Don't allow merchants to lodge outside the city.
Jeremiah 17:19-27	Don't bear a burden. Don't carry a burden in the into the city gates. Don't carry a burden out of your house.
Amos 8:4-5	Don't sell grain or offer wheat for sale.

These are all the things that are specifically called out in SCRIPTURE as a violation of Shabbat. So does that mean that these are the only things that violate Shabbat? Does that mean that as long you aren't doing one of these specific things that you won't be breaking Shabbat? Or is there more to it than that?

The saying is true: "Give a man a fish and you have fed him for a day. But teach a man to fish and you will feed him for a lifetime." This summary of the individual and specific prohibitions on Shabbat is meant to teach you to fish. Because if you see the common themes and recurring principles in these prohibitions that *are* found in SCRIPTURE, then you will be able to apply these principles to your life for things that *are not* found in SCRIPTURE. If you find yourself wondering, "Am I allowed to do this on Shabbat?" or "Is this good to do on Shabbat?" but there is no chapter and verse in SCRIPTURE to refer to for that specific situation, what will you do? You are not always going to be able to find a SCRIPTURE verse for literally every situation in life. So, for the things that SCRIPTURE does not mention specifically, it is better to understand these principles for yourself so that you can apply them yourself. In that way, you will learn how to fish instead of having to receive another fish from someone else every time.

Remember that the goal here in teaching you how to fish is not that you would ever add to what SCRIPTURE already says. Never do that. If you ever discover that your application of keeping Shabbat is in violation of other Commandments from SCRIPTURE, then you know that your interpretation and application cannot be correct. But the goal of teaching you how to fish is so that you will know what GOD'S Will is and what would be pleasing to HIM in any given scenario concerning Shabbat that is not specifically mentioned in SCRIPTURE. Neither are these principles meant to replace the Commandments of GOD concerning Shabbat in SCRIPTURE in any way. Rather, they are to help you understand what might be the reason why HE gave such Commandments in the first place.

Almost every one of these prohibitions can be boiled down to these two themes or principles:

- Don't do any kind of regular work or anything that could be mentally or physically tiring.

- Don't do anything to gather for yourself or build your own kingdom or seek your own gain, profit, benefit, or increase.

And even these two themes could be combined into this one: Don't enslave yourself for the sake of building your own temporary kingdom because HE has already given you an inheritance in HIS Everlasting Kingdom.

Compare these principles for Shabbat with Isaiah 55:1-3.

1. What do you do when you need guidance in any decision but there is nothing in SCRIPTURE about it?

   _____

   _____

   _____

2. Can you see how these two principles describe all the prohibitions concerning Shabbat in SCRIPTURE?

   _____

   _____

   _____

3. Does seeing these similarities and recurring themes throughout the Shabbat prohibitions reveal to you something about THE LORD that you may not have known before?

   _____

   _____

   _____

Additional Notes:

_____

_____

_____

_____

_____

_____

_____

Leviticus 19:9-10
Leviticus 23:22
Deuteronomy 23:24-25
Matthew 11:27-12:14
Mark 2:23-3:6
Luke 6:1-11
Luke 13:10-17
Luke 14:1-24
John 5:5-18
John 9:1-16

7.5 Did YESHUA Keep The Sabbath?

It's a fair question. It seems like the pharisees and sadducees were always accusing YESHUA and HIS Disciples of breaking The Sabbath in The Gospels. So did YESHUA keep The Sabbath? And if HE did, how did HE keep it? At this point, some of you BIBLE scholars might be saying, "Wait a minute. Didn't JESUS admit to working on The Sabbath?" It is true that in John 5:16-18 YESHUA says, "My FATHER is working until now, and I am working" in regard to what HE was doing on Shabbat. But what was HE doing on Shabbat? And exactly what was HE admitting to doing? Let's take a look. These are all the things they accused HIM and or HIS Disciples of doing to break Shabbat.

Matthew 12:1-8 Mark 2:23-28 Luke 6:1-5	HIS Disciples picking individual heads of grain and eating them.
Matthew 12:9-14 Mark 3:1-6 Luke 6:6-11	Healing a man's withered hand.
Luke 13:10-17	Healing a woman from a disabling spirit.
Luke 14:16	Healing a man from dropsy or swelling.
John 5:5-18	Healing an invalid of 38 years.
John 9:1-16	Healing a man from lifelong blindness.

As you can see, almost every time they falsely accuse HIM of violating Shabbat, it's specifically because HE healed someone. The only time when this is not the case is when The Disciples were plucking heads of grain and eating them on Shabbat. So since this instance is unique among all the other false accusations, let's deal with that one first.

In Matthew 12:13, Mark 2:23-24, and Luke 6:1-2, the pharisees accuse YESHUA'S Disciples to HIM of doing what they say is unlawful on Shabbat. But in Leviticus 19:9-10 and Leviticus 23:22, THE WORD says not to reap a field entirely but to leave the edge or corner of the field to be gleaned by the poor and the sojourner. The Disciples followed YESHUA day and night. They were with HIM all the time. They did not often have a means to provide for themselves. So, this provision in SCRIPTURE would have been for them. And if that wasn't enough, Deuteronomy 23:24-25 makes allowance for exactly what The Disciples were doing. What better time for the poor and hungry to come and be filled than The Sabbath? It would be a different matter if they were harvesting the field. If they had gone out there with sickles and started cutting down bundles, throwing them over their shoulders or onto carts and hauling them away, then it would not be surprising or wrong for the pharisees to say that The Disciples were violating Shabbat. But that's not what they were doing. They were simply plucking individual heads of grain for the sake of their own hunger—something that is completely lawful to do on Shabbat according to SCRIPTURE.

Now back to John 5:16-18. In this passage YESHUA says, "My FATHER is working until now, and I am working." At first glance it may seem like HE is admitting a violation of Shabbat, but after reading what is Written in the previously listed passages, we will soon see that is not the case.

HE admitted to "working" not to violating Shabbat. And clearly healing someone with a spoken Word is not the same kind of work as what most people would call work. Take a second to compare the two lists laid out in this chapter. You will find that the contents of the two are completely different from one another. The first is a list of all the things that GOD HIMSELF calls violations of Shabbat from The Old Covenant SCRIPTURES. These are all things that people did in selfishness and for their own personal preference, gain, or benefit. The second list is made up of all the things YESHUA was accused of violating the Sabbath for. All these things HE did completely selflessly and for the sake of other people's benefit, healing, and even their Salvation. In fact, I think it is safe to say that if HE had not said HE was working, no one but the pharisees and sadducees would have considered it to be work.

Yes, HE admitted to the work of healing someone on Shabbat. But in the case of the man with the withered hand, the scribes and pharisees are trying to make the same accusation against HIM. It is in response to that accusation that HE says in Matthew 12:12, "So it is lawful to do good on the Sabbath." And when we read of the same event in both Mark's and Luke's GOSPELS, HE asks them a very intentional question. In both Mark 3:4 and Luke 6:9, HE asked them, "Is it lawful on the Sabbath to do good or to do harm, to save life or to kill?" HE was obviously looking for a specific answer and trying to lead them to admit that it is lawful to do good on Shabbat.

And the case of the woman with a disabling spirit that YESHUA healed on Shabbat is really the icing on the cake. In Luke 13:16 YESHUA says to the ruler of the synagogue, "And ought not this woman, a daughter of Abraham whom satan bound for eighteen years, be loosed from this bond on the Sabbath day?" Just for emphasis and to drive the point home, let's temporarily remove the descriptive middle part of this verse so that we're only left with the beginning and ending of the verse. Then it would read like this: "And ought not this woman . . . be loosed from this bond on the Sabbath day?" HE is basically saying that this woman absolutely should be healed on The Sabbath specifically because it is The Sabbath. In order to understand why HE says this about Shabbat, take another look at verse 12 and zoom in on and remember the word "freed." This is very significant and will be important in later chapters.

So it may seem at first glance that YESHUA is admitting to violating Shabbat in John 5:16-18. But it's easy to see from these other verses that what HE actually means by what HE says in John 5:16-18 is, "I am doing this work because it's completely lawful to do on The Sabbath, and in fact it should be done on The Sabbath." Now, we come back to the original question: Did YESHUA keep Shabbat? Yes. Not only did GOD'S SON keep Shabbat, but HE also showed all the hypocritical religious leaders around HIM how they should be keeping Shabbat.

1. After reading through this study and the SCRIPTURE
    verses in it, what are some things that you could say are
    completely lawful to do on Shabbat?

    _____

    _____

    _____

2. What do these verses from Leviticus and Deuteronomy in
    this study say to you about the Goodness of GOD?

    _____

    _____

    _____

3. Does this list of things that YESHUA did on Shabbat tell you
    anything about how THE LORD sees Shabbat and how we
    should keep it?

    _____

    _____

    _____

Additional Notes:

_____

_____

_____

_____

_____

_____

_____

Is Keeping Shabbat Important to GOD?

Exodus 31:12-17
Importance.
Punishment.

Exodus 35:1-3
Punishment.

Leviticus 19:1-4
Importance.

Leviticus 26:1-2
Importance.

Numbers 15:30-36
Punishment.

Nehemiah 1:1-3
A Promise Fulfilled.

Nehemiah 13:15-22
Severity.
Punishment.

Isaiah 56:1-8
Importance.
Reward.

Isaiah 58:6-14
Reward.

Jeremiah 17:19-27
Severity.
Punishment.
Reward.

Ezekiel 20:10-26
Importance.
Punishment.

Ezekiel 22:6-16
Severity.
Punishment.

Ezekiel 22:26-31
Severity.
Punishment.

Amos 8:1-10
Punishment.

Colossians 2:13-17
No Judgment.

Introduction to Chapter 8
An Obvious Answer

Yes, it is. At this point, it could seem like a somewhat ridiculous question. But the reason for posing the question and really the whole point of this entire book is to help GOD'S People understand exactly how important keeping Shabbat is to THE LORD and why. It is not my intent to make anyone feel judged or condemned if they have never observed Shabbat before. Rather, the purpose is to help people see and understand and begin to have a desire of their own to keep The Sabbath Holy in their personal walk with THE LORD. Because if keeping the Sabbath is important to Our FATHER, then it is important to us. And the best way to find out exactly how important it is to HIM is to examine the way HE speaks about HIS Holy day, the kind of punishments HE gives for violating Shabbat, and the kind of rewards HE gives for keeping and honoring Shabbat in HIS WORD. In this chapter, we will be doing just that.

Exodus 31:12-17
Exodus 35:1-3
Numbers 15:30-36
Nehemiah 1:1-3
Nehemiah 13:15-22
Jeremiah 17:19-27
Ezekiel 20:10-26
Ezekiel 22:6-16
Ezekiel 22:26-31
Amos 8:1-10

8.1 The Severity of Violating The Sabbath and the Punishment for It

By taking a closer look at Ezekiel 22:6-12 and Ezekiel 22:26-29, we can see that profaning The Sabbath is not something THE LORD takes lightly. This becomes very obvious very quickly when we see that the sin of profaning The Sabbath finds a place among all the other terrible sins listed in these two passages. In these two passages GOD is naming and listing all the sins for which HE is punishing and bringing wrath on HIS People. These lists include sins like extortion, treating their Fathers and Mothers with contempt, taking bribes to shed blood, making wives into widows, adultery, and several kinds of incest. And the sin of profaning The Sabbath is counted among these sins. GOD even says in Ezekiel 22:26, "they have disregarded my Sabbaths, so that I am profaned among them." In Nehemiah 13:15 and also in verse 21, Nehemiah is warning The People not to violate Shabbat. In verse 17 He calls what they were doing "profaning The Sabbath" and an "evil thing." Nehemiah did not say, "maybe consider not doing what you're doing because it's kinda not good." No. He said, "What is this evil thing you are doing, profaning the Sabbath day?" And in Jeremiah 17:19-27, THE LORD HIMSELF is issuing a warning to The People not to violate Shabbat. HE begins this warning in verse 21 by saying, "take care for the sake of your lives."

These are only the things GOD has said about profaning Shabbat. Now let's take a look at what HE has done about it. As we begin to discuss the punishments THE LORD dealt out for profaning Shabbat, it seems very appropriate to separate these punishments into two different categories and consider these punishments according to those categories. The two categories are **personal punishment** (punishments that are only dealt to individuals) and **national punishment** (punishments that are dealt to the entire Nation). The difference between the two is very important because a nation is made up of individuals. And the fact of the matter is that hundreds of years before GOD ever gave any warnings through the Prophets concerning national punishment, HE first gave them instructions in HIS TORAH for how to deal with personal punishment for this sin. If The People had been faithful to obey The Commandments concerning personal punishment, then the rest of The People would have seen what happened to those individuals and would have been careful to not replicate their actions in violating Shabbat. And so if they had obeyed The Commandments concerning personal punishment, there would never have been any need for national punishment concerning this particular sin. Our LORD is THE MOST WISE KING in the way that HE structures HIS KINGDOM. Remember this concept and the relationship between the two categories as we begin to discuss these punishments.

A brief side note: It is important to mention that profaning Shabbat is only one of the sins for which GOD brought such punishments on The People. This Judgment wasn't given solely because of violating Shabbat, but that was one of the reasons for it. And it is easier to make mention of that here once rather than make mention of it every time we discuss one of these specific punishments. Now back to the study.

Let's start with the personal punishments since they appear first in SCRIPTURE. In both Exodus 31:14-15 and Exodus 35:2, there is very clear instruction that anyone who violates Shabbat is to be put to death. And in Numbers 15:30-36, we see an example of this being carried out with the man who was stoned to death outside The Camp. Whether some of The People who witnessed this punishment took warning or not, it is evident from the SCRIPTURE verses we are about to discuss that most of The People of that generation as well as future generations did not heed that warning. Now let's take a look at some of the national Judgments that happened as a result of neglecting the personal punishment.

In Ezekiel 20:21-24 and Ezekiel 22:15-16, THE LORD tells HIS People that HE will scatter them among the Nations and that they will be profaned in the sight of the Nations. We know from both THE BIBLE and history that GOD'S People definitely were scattered among the Nations through the Babylonian captivity and through other means. But how were they profaned in the sight of the Nations? In Amos 8:10 we can see exactly how. It is easy to see how the punishments and misfortunes listed in this verse would be a profaning and a humiliation to anyone in the sight of surrounding Nations. In Jeremiah 17:27, THE LORD Says to the inhabitants of Jerusalem that if they don't listen to HIM and begin to keep Shabbat Holy, HE will "kindle a fire in its gates, and it shall devour the palaces of Jerusalem." And both Ezekiel 22:31 and Nehemiah 1:1-3 clearly verify that is exactly what HE did. Because in Ezekiel 22:31, HE Says "I *have consumed* them with the fire of my wrath" in past tense, meaning that HE has already done it. And if that wasn't enough, in Nehemiah 1:1-3, Hanani comes to inform Nehemiah that Jerusalem's Gates are destroyed by fire. Is it any wonder why later in Nehemiah 13:17-18 Nehemiah says that profaning Shabbat is what their ancestors did to bring wrath and disaster from GOD? He had already seen the results of it once, and He didn't want it to happen again.

1. If you were to summarize, what do you think these verses suggest about how THE LORD feels about HIS People violating HIS Sabbath?

    _____

    _____

    _____

2. Does the concept of personal punishment in contrast to national punishment affect the way you think about the crime rate in your own country?

    _____

    _____

    _____

3. Can you think of any ways that concept could be applied to prevent the overall morale decay of the public?

    _____

    _____

    _____

Additional Notes:

_____

_____

_____

_____

_____

_____

Exodus 31:12-17
Leviticus 19:1-4
Leviticus 26:1-2
Isaiah 56:1-8
Isaiah 58:6-14
Jeremiah 17:19-27
Ezekiel 20:10-26

8.2 *The Importance of Keeping The Sabbath and the Reward for It*

In this study we will see a comparison that is very similar to the one in the previous section. We have already seen the kind of emphasis THE LORD puts on "not profaning Shabbat" by the severity of the sins that "profaning Shabbat" is listed among. In the same way, the importance of "keeping Shabbat" is indicated by the importance of the other Commandments that "keeping Shabbat" is listed among. In both Leviticus 19:1-4 and Leviticus 26:1-2, the Commandment or Instruction to keep THE LORD'S Sabbath is found right alongside other Commandments such as not making or bowing down to idols, revering one's Mother and Father, being Holy because GOD is HOLY, and revering GOD'S Sanctuary.

It is so important to HIM that in Ezekiel 20:18-21, HE actually tells the children to disobey their pagan parents in order to keep HIS Rules and HIS Sabbaths. This is a very big deal. Anyone who has ever read SCRIPTURE before knows that honoring and respecting one's Parents is one of GOD'S Ten Commandments and therefore is itself very important to GOD. The fact that HE tells these children to disobey their parents for the sake of keeping Shabbat ought to really grab our attention. It definitely brings Exodus 31:12-13 into perspective. Many versions of SCRIPTURE translate verse 13 to say, "*surely* you shall keep my Sabbaths" or "*most certainly* you shall keep my Sabbaths." But the English Standard Version translates verse 13 as "*above all* you shall keep my Sabbaths."

And again, the things GOD has said about keeping Shabbat are backed up by the rewards and blessings for keeping Shabbat. In Isaiah 56:1-8, Isaiah 58:13-14, and Jeremiah 17:24-26, GOD gives incredible blessings for keeping Shabbat Holy. By reading through these verses carefully, you will see that most of these blessings specifically have to do with THE TEMPLE, with Kingship, and with a Priesthood. Remember this concept because it will be important in later chapters.

1. If you were to summarize, what do you think these passages suggest about how THE LORD feels about HIS People keeping HIS Sabbath Holy?

    _____

    _____

    _____

2. If the children in Ezekiel 20:18-21 had to disobey their parents in order to keep Shabbat, what does that say about their parents?

    _____

    _____

    _____

3. Based on the context of Isaiah 56:1-8, are the rewards for keeping Shabbat only for The Jewish People or for everyone?

    _____

    _____

    _____

Additional Notes:

_____

_____

_____

_____

_____

_____

_____

The Weightier Matters of Shabbat

Up to this point, we have covered a lot about the simple application of keeping Shabbat. But many times throughout SCRIPTURE, THE LORD will give a simple instruction in order to teach us about something else.

For example, THE TEMPLE (which is made of three compartments) is an illustration and teaching about how our bodies are also tripartite (spirit, soul, and body). The indwelling of THE HOLY SPIRIT and everything that went on in THE TEMPLE during its regular function is a picture and a teaching about what would happen to our bodies at the moment of conversion when THE HOLY SPIRIT comes to indwell us.

That's just one example of how THE LORD will use simple things in SCRIPTURE to teach us greater Truths. And The Sabbath is definitely one of those things. So throughout the next four chapters, we will be approaching the subject of Shabbat from a different angle in order to answer different kinds of questions. Questions such as:

- What are the weightier matters of Shabbat?
- What do these instructions about Shabbat really mean?
- Is there something more to it?
- What was THE LORD trying to teach us through the institution of Shabbat?
- Does The Sabbath have any Prophetic implications to it?

These are the things we will be looking into in the next several chapters.

CHAPTER 9

A Holy Convocation

Leviticus 23:1-3
A Holy Convocation.

Deuteronomy 8:2-3
Not By Bread Alone But By Every WORD OF GOD.

2 Kings 4:18-23
The Usual Time To Go Before God.

Psalm 92:1-15
A Psalm for The Sabbath.

Proverbs 18:1
He who isolates himself.

Isaiah 55:1-3
A Time Of Fellowship With THE LORD At HIS Table.

Ezekiel 2:9-3:3
Take and eat THE WORD OF GOD.

Ezekiel 45:13-17
A Holy Convocation.

Ezekiel 46:1-5
Draw Near To Worship GOD.

Matthew 4:1-4
Not By Bread Alone But By Every WORD OF GOD.

Mark 1:21-31
Come And Hear The WORD OF GOD.

Mark 6:1-2
Come And Hear the WORD OF GOD.

Luke 4:1-4
Not By Bread Alone But By Every WORD OF GOD.

Luke 4:14-22
Come And Hear THE WORD OF GOD.

Luke 4:31-39
Come And Hear THE WORD OF GOD.

Luke 13:10-17
Come And Hear THE WORD OF GOD.

Luke 14:1-24
A Time Of Fellowship With THE LORD At His Table.

John 1:1-4
In the beginning was THE WORD

John 4:5-34
The Unseen Water And The Unseen Bread.

John 6:22-68
True Food And True Drink. Eat, Drink, And Live.

Acts 13:13-48
Come And Hear THE WORD OF GOD.

Acts 15:21
Come And Hear THE WORD OF GOD.

Acts 16:13
Draw Near To Worship GOD.

Acts 17:2-4
Come And Hear THE WORD OF GOD.

Acts 18:4-5
Come and Hear THE WORD OF GOD.

Romans 12:1-2
A Living Sacrifice.

Hebrews 10:19-25
Do Not Forsake The Assembly.

Revelation 1:10
The Usual Time To Go Before GOD. Draw Near To Worship GOD.

Revelation 10:1-11
Take and eat THE WORD OF GOD.

Revelation 19:11-16
HIS NAME is THE WORD OF GOD.

Introduction to Chapter 9
So What Are We Supposed to Do?

So far, we have covered a lot about the prohibitions of Shabbat and all the things we're not supposed to do on The Sabbath. But what are some of the things that we are supposed to do on Shabbat? What does THE LORD require of us on Shabbat, and what does Our FATHER want to do with HIS Holy Day? In this chapter, we will attempt to answer those questions.

Leviticus 23:1-3
2 Kings 4:18-23
Proverbs 18:1
Ezekiel 45:13-17
Ezekiel 46:1-5
Hebrews 10:19-25

9.1 What's a Convocation?

It is commanded by THE LORD in Leviticus 23:1-3 that Shabbat is to be a Holy Convocation. But what exactly is a ***convocation***? The original Hebrew word in SCRIPTURE that is translated into English as ***convocation*** is the word מקרא which is pronounced ***miqra***. This word ***miqra*** has a two-part meaning. The first part is "a gathering or an assembling of all the People," which is why some translations of SCRIPTURE use the phrase "Sacred Assembly" instead of "Holy Convocation."

And that is exactly what Shabbat has always been ever since Creation. It has always been a time for all of GOD'S People to gather or assemble before HIM. And there are many verses in SCRIPTURE to verify this concept. In both Ezekiel 45:16-17 and Ezekiel 46:3, it is plain to see that ***all*** The People are involved with bringing Offerings and Worshiping THE LORD at THE TEMPLE on Shabbat. In 2 Kings 4:23, the Husband of the Shunammite woman is actually puzzled as to why She would go to The Man of GOD on a day other than The Sabbath because The Sabbath is the usual time for GOD'S People to meet with HIM. And in Hebrews 10:25, The Apostle Paul is giving a very clear instruction not to forsake the assembly.

Despite verses like these, there are still many people who believe they can legitimately keep Shabbat by themselves alone in their houses. Not only is this idea unBIBLICAL, but it is also a very unhealthy choice for anyone's walk with THE LORD, and the reasons for this will become obvious in the following studies presented in this chapter. If you need convincing before then, just make a quick reference to Proverbs 18:1.

1. In your own words, what would you say makes the convocation Holy?

   _____

   _____

   _____

2. Can you think of any reasons why THE LORD wants us to assemble before HIM?

   _____

   _____

   _____

3. Why would THE LORD not want you personally to forsake the assembly?

   _____

   _____

   _____

Additional Notes:

   _____

   _____

   _____

   _____

   _____

   _____

   _____

Psalm 92:1-15
Ezekiel 45:13-17
Ezekiel 46:1-5
Acts 16:13
Romans 12:1-2
Revelation 1:10

9.2 *Why Do We Assemble Before HIM?*

We have discussed that Shabbat is meant to be an Assembly or a gathering together of Believers before GOD. But why? What do we do when we are all gathered before HIM? There are at least two reasons for gathering. The first is corporate Worship. Your Offering of Worship may be in Song or Praise or Thanksgiving or Prayer or a combination of all these. But do not show up in HIS PRESENCE empty-handed. We should all come before HIM with the Worship of HIS GREAT NAME.

In Ezekiel 45:13-17 all The People are Worshiping THE LORD on Shabbat with the physical Offerings of wheat, barley, oil, and sheep that they bring to THE TEMPLE. But in many places in SCRIPTURE, things like Song, Praise, Thanksgiving, and Prayer are called Offerings. By comparing this concept to Psalm 92:1-5, you will find something very interesting. The beginning of Psalm 92:1-5 says that this Psalm is "a song for The Sabbath." And three of those four methods of Worship are directly mentioned in Psalm 92:1-5. So Ezekiel 45:13-17 is an example of physical Worship, and Psalm 92:1-5 is an example of Spiritual Worship.

Ezekiel 46:3 says that on The Sabbath, the People of The Land will bow down before THE LORD at the entrance of The Gate. In Acts 16:13 we can see that The Apostle Paul and those with Him were seeking a place of Prayer on Shabbat, and in Revelation 1:10, John The Revelator says He "was in THE SPIRIT on THE LORD'S Day." Each one of these methods of Worship is a great example of how we should be relating to and entering into fellowship with our FATHER every day, but especially on Shabbat. And a careful examination of these verses really brings Romans 12:1-2 into perspective.

1. What would you say is the biggest difference between the physical worship and the spiritual worship?

   _____

   _____

   _____

2. Do you think THE LORD would rather receive cattle, grain, and wine or you as an offering?

   _____

   _____

   _____

3. What are some ways that you can offer spiritual worship to THE LORD?

   _____

   _____

   _____

Additional Notes:

_____

_____

_____

_____

_____

_____

_____

Leviticus 23:1-3
Mark 1:21-31
Mark 6:1-2
Luke 4:14-22
Luke 4:31-39
Luke 13:10-17
Acts 13:13-48
Acts 15:21
Acts 17:2-4
Acts 18:4-5

9.3 Hear THE WORD Proclaimed

And what is the second reason why we gather before HIM? The second reason is also the second part of the definition of the word *miqra* or *convocation*. A convocation is not only a gathering, but it is a gathering for the purpose of a message being proclaimed and heard by all The People. To convocate means to assemble and hear. In other words, the main purpose of the Holy Convocation that THE LORD Commands us to keep on Shabbat in Leviticus 23:1-3 is for GOD'S People to come together to hear THE WORD OF GOD proclaimed.

All five of the passages from both Mark and Luke listed above basically repeat the same thing—that it was YESHUA'S habit to go into the synagogue on Shabbat to read and teach SCRIPTURE. What an amazing thought. THE WORD OF GOD stood up to read and teach THE WORD OF GOD. It appears from THE GOSPELS that HE did this in every synagogue in every town HE went to.

It is easy to see from both Acts 17:2-4 and Acts 18:4-5 that The Apostle Paul did the same thing. Acts 13:44 says, "The next Sabbath almost the whole city gathered to hear THE WORD OF THE LORD." Now that's a convocation! Ever since the time when GOD'S People first assembled at the base of Mt. Sinai up until today, THE WORD OF GOD has always been read, proclaimed, and taught wherever GOD'S People come together on The Sabbath. And we can easily see that verified by Acts 13:27 and Acts 15:21.

1. Are you facing anything in your life right now that is forcing you to stop and hear THE LORD?

   _____

   _____

   _____

2. How often do you gather with other believers to hear THE WORD OF GOD?

   _____

   _____

   _____

3. What kind of things do you think THE LORD might proclaim through you if you stopped to hear HIM?

   _____

   _____

   _____

Additional Notes:

   _____

   _____

   _____

   _____

   _____

   _____

   _____

Deuteronomy 8:2-3
Isaiah 55:1-3
Ezekiel 2:9-3:3
Matthew 4:1-4
Luke 4:1-4
Luke 14:1-24
John 1:1-4
John 4:5-34
John 6:22-68
Revelation 10:1-11
Revelation 19:11-16

9.4 Fellowship with THE LORD at HIS Table

It has been a long-standing tradition for those of GOD'S People who keep Shabbat to begin their Sabbath on friday night with Prayer, gathered around a dinner table with Family and a warm meal. There is no specific Command in SCRIPTURE to keep Shabbat in this way. But is there any BIBLICAL significance to such a tradition? We have already discussed the main three things we are to do on Shabbat, which are gather before HIM, Worship HIM, and hear from HIS WORD. But what do those things have to do with Family around a dinner table? Let's find out.

Both Matthew 4:1-4 and Luke 4:1-4 give account of YESHUA'S temptation in the wilderness by the enemy. And in both accounts, when the enemy tempts HIM, HE responds by quoting Deuteronomy 8:2-3 when HE says, "Man shall not live by bread alone, but by every word that comes from the mouth of GOD." And HE tells HIS Disciples something very similar in John 4:30-34 when HE says, "I have food to eat that you do not know about" and "My food is to do the will of him who sent me and to accomplish his work." In both scenarios HE was already hungry when someone tried to get HIM to eat food. In both scenarios,

HIS answer indicated that hearing and doing THE WORD OF GOD was HIS food and that it was more capable of sustaining HIM than any physical food.

HE speaks this way about the necessity of us ingesting THE WORD OF GOD for good reason. It is not just a metaphor; it is a literal spiritual reality. This spiritual reality of THE WORD OF GOD is just as true and relevant for us today as it was for our MESSIAH back then. Both The Prophet Ezekiel and John The Revelator experienced this spiritual reality in a whole new way when they were told to "eat this scroll" in Ezekiel 2:9-3:3 and Revelation 10:1-11, respectively. Again these events were not metaphorical; these two men in THE SPIRIT actually ate scrolls with GOD'S WORDS on them so that they could speak them back out in accordance with GOD'S Will.

Have you ever entered into a time of Prayer, Fasting, and SCRIPTURE reading when you didn't eat or drink anything, but somehow you never actually felt hungry, and you felt more alive and more energized than you ever did before you started? That's because THE WORD OF GOD is literally food for your Soul and Spirit, and YESHUA HIMSELF is that very WORD.

In both John 1:1 and Revelation 19:13, we are reminded of exactly who YESHUA is. HE is THE WORD OF GOD. That is HIS NAME, HIS IDENTITY, and HIS RENOWN. This same WORD is our Spiritual food from GOD. YESHUA verifies this in both John 4:7-15 and John 6:27-58. In John 4:7-15 HE is telling the Woman at the well in no uncertain terms that HE is the source of and the giver of LIVING WATER. And in John 6:27-58 HE describes HIMSELF by saying things like, "I am the bread of life" and "my flesh is true food and my blood is true drink." Remember that Shabbat is a time to gather before THE LORD and hear HIS WORD proclaimed.

Now compare all this to Isaiah 55:1-3 and Luke 14:1-24. The metaphor used in Isaiah 55:1-3 is clear enough and can be summed up this way: Come to THE LORD because HIS WORD is good food for you. But that's not all this passage is about, and these are not random instructions. Rather these instructions in

Isaiah 55:2-3 are metaphoric equations to one another. In other words, to "incline your ear" to HIM is to "come to" HIM. And to "hear" HIM and "listen diligently to" HIM is to "eat what is good" and "delight yourselves in rich food that your soul may live." And in Luke 14:1-24 YESHUA takes HIS seat at a table on Shabbat and begins to teach everyone at that table THE WORD OF THE LORD. By doing this, HE set before them what is "true food" and "true drink."

So, back to the original question: What does keeping Shabbat have to do with Prayer, Family, and a warm meal around a dinner table? Let me try to explain it like this. At the end of a long week, at the beginning of Shabbat, a FATHER takes HIS seat at the head of the table. And one after another, all HIS Children *convocate* around the table with their eyes fixed on THE FATHER. They **Pray** to THE FATHER, saying things like: "Oh FATHER it's been such a long and troubled week, but I'm so glad to finally see YOU and be here in YOUR PRESENCE." And They begin to **Worship** HIM and enjoy a time of close Fellowship with THE FATHER. THE FATHER then sets on the table before them THE WORDS OF LIFE, THE BREAD OF LIFE, LIVING WATER, NEW WINE, and THE OIL OF GLADNESS so that The Children may eat Their fill and be satisfied in HIM.

1. What do you think about the way these passages speak about THE WORD OF GOD and what does it mean for us as HIS People today?

   _____

   _____

   _____

2. Which one of the Spiritual Foods named in the last sentence of this study are you lacking in or starving for?

   _____

   _____

   _____

3. How do you plan to have that need satisfied?

   _____

   _____

   _____

Additional Notes:

   _____

   _____

   _____

   _____

   _____

   _____

   _____

CHAPTER 10

Don't Keep Shabbat Hypocritically

Exodus 20:8-11
Remember Shabbat. Shabbat is for everyone.

Exodus 23:9-12
Shabbat is for everyone.

Leviticus 19:30
Reverence for the things of GOD.

Deuteronomy 5:12-15
Shabbat is for everyone. Remember why you keep Shabbat.

Deuteronomy 6:4-9
THE LORD and HIS WORDS should be the subject
of conversation on Shabbat.

Deuteronomy 11:18-20
THE LORD and HIS WORDS should be the subject
of conversation on Shabbat.

Nehemiah 13:15-22
Way too eager for Shabbat to be over.

Isaiah 1:11-17
Does GOD hate The Assembly on Shabbat or the sin in it?

Isaiah 58:6-14
Refrain from doing what you want and still call Shabbat a delight.

Amos 8:1-10
Way too eager for Shabbat to be over.

Matthew 7:12
Give rest to others as it has been given to you.

Mark 12:28-34
The greatest commandment.

Luke 13:10-17
Why did YESHUA call them hypocrites?

Introduction to Chapter 10
What Do You Mean "Hypocritically?"

So what is a hypocrite anyway? Most of the ways in which the word *hypocrite* is used in conversation nowadays don't really convey the meaning very well. Hypocrisy is more than just a self-contradicting standard; that is only a result or a symptom of the root problem of hypocrisy. The English word *hypocrite* is a transliteration of a Greek word that means "an actor, a stage player, one who puts on a mask or many masks, or one who is a counterfeit." Or to put it in a more modern definition, it means "to be fake." A hypocrite wants to appear to be one way in public while in reality they are another way in private. A hypocrite wants to appear to be one way as an outer facade while they are an entirely different way in their heart and mind.

How do we make sure we're not doing that with Shabbat? By this point, we've discussed most of the physical and external dos and don'ts of keeping Shabbat. But what about the internal? What kind of attitude and mentality should we have about Shabbat itself and about keeping it? What kind of motive should we have to keep Shabbat? These are the things we will be discussing in this chapter.

Nehemiah 13:15-22
Isaiah 1:11-17
Isaiah 58:6-14
Amos 8:1-10
Luke 13:10-17

10.1 The Wrong Attitude and Priority

Most of the time, people will identify hypocrisy in another person by that person's actions. And they are not entirely wrong in identifying it this way. Isaiah 1:11-17 is a good example of this. If someone were to read verses 13-14 of this passage carelessly and without paying attention, they could easily come away with an impression and interpretation that GOD hates the Sabbath Assembly. Because THE LORD HIMSELF says in verse 14 "Your new moons and your appointed feasts my soul hates," and The Sabbath is one of the appointed feasts.

This ought to make us stop and think for a moment. Why would THE ONE who instituted Shabbat hate Shabbat? The short answer is "HE doesn't." The longer answer is this. Notice HE says, "*Your* new moons and *your* appointed feasts my soul hates". In other words, when THE LORD said this, HE was specifically speaking to The People of that particular generation. That statement is not addressed to anyone today who has a desire to keep The Sabbath, so it should not be used as such unless it applies. The reason HE said this to them is because their lives were full of sin and iniquity, and they were coming to celebrate HIS Sabbaths and other Holy Days like there was no sin problem and everything was just fine. In other words, they were keeping Shabbat in blatant hypocrisy and the context of this passage plainly shows that. GOD hated the sin and iniquity in *their* assembly and the way *they* were doing it, not the assembly itself. So in this example, it's easy enough to see that their actions were an indication of their hypocrisy. But it is important to remember that although hypocrisy can be identified in one's actions, it never begins in their actions but in their heart.

Nehemiah 13:15-22 and Amos 8:1-10 are two of the most obvious examples that we have in SCRIPTURE of having a wrong heart and a wrong attitude toward Shabbat. But the hypocrite that YESHUA is speaking to in Luke 13:10-17 isn't quite as easy to spot because his hypocrisy is hiding behind a supposed concern for Shabbat. But these first two passages are painfully obvious and have this in common: The people described in both passages just can't wait for Shabbat to be over. The first one is showing it through their actions, and the second one is showing it through their words, but they are both showing an incredible lack of appreciation and even disdain for GOD'S Holy Day. Why were they so eager for Shabbat to be over? Because they had set making money and their own business sales as a higher priority than spending time in THE PRESENCE OF THE LORD and honoring HIM on HIS Holy Day. Don't be like them.

In Isaiah 58:13-14 we find one of the best examples of what GOD thinks about Shabbat and about us keeping it, but verse 13 is very interesting. Most versions of SCRIPTURE will translate the end of this verse as saying, "not talking idly" or "not speaking your own words." But there are at least three versions that translate it as "not talking business" or "not making business deals" or "not speaking about business." It is important to note that most versions of SCRIPTURE do not translate the verse this way and these three versions are definitely in the minority. And so, you wouldn't be able to honestly point someone to this verse in order to say, "See?! You shouldn't be talking about business on Shabbat!"

Nevertheless, the concept and theme of such an interpretation goes hand in hand with what the rest of SCRIPTURE says about Shabbat. And it is true that You attend a Shabbat gathering to focus on, Pray to, give Glory to, Worship, and be with THE LORD. If you are doing those things, you probably won't be thinking about price tags or purchases. And if you aren't thinking about those things, you won't be talking about them. It is best to stay away from such conversation on HIS Holy Day.

It is not uncommon for most people nowadays to constantly be checking the time to see how much longer they will be in

Church or Synagogue because they can't wait for it to be over. They want it to look like from their physical attendance to that particular building that they are dedicated to THE LORD. But that is only an outer appearance. What's really going on in their mind and heart is impatience and indifference toward GOD. Again, don't be like them. I can assure you that whatever it is that you're so anxious to do when you leave isn't anywhere near as important as what you could be doing while you're there. You could be seeking THE PRESENCE OF GOD. You could be eating from THE BREAD OF LIFE and drinking from THE WELL OF SALVATION. That brings us to the next passage of SCRIPTURE.

Why exactly did YESHUA call the ruler of The Synagogue a hypocrite in Luke 13:10-17? The short answer is that the ruler's religious legalism was causing him to treat his own livestock better than GOD'S Children. But there's more to it than that. As mentioned before, he wanted to appear to everyone around him that what he was saying was out of concern for Shabbat. But both what he said and the reasoning that led to what he said are about as anti-Sabbath as he could possibly be.

My personal suspicion is that a big part of the reason why the ruler of The Synagogue said this was because he wasn't the center of attention while YESHUA was healing this Woman. I also suspect that he may have been thinking about the fact that no one he prayed for ever got healed. Both attitudes would be inappropriate because Shabbat is supposed to be all about GOD and not this ruler of The Synagogue. But my hunches and suspicions are not SCRIPTURE. So, let's take a look at what the text actually says.

This Woman came to Synagogue on Shabbat and received a Miraculous healing from GOD. What happened to this Woman is very similar to what happened to the ox or donkey. Think about it. On Shabbat the ox or donkey was *untied* and led away to a place where it could *drink water*. Let's put it in other terms. The animal was *unbound* and brought to a *place of rest* where it could *receive nourishment*. That is exactly what we all should be hoping for when we come to Shabbat. It is a time to set our burdens down and come to receive refreshment from THE LORD. And that is exactly what this Woman received.

And this ruler of The Synagogue apparently had an understanding of this when it came to his animals but not when it came to GOD'S Children. He didn't at all seem to be concerned with this disabled Woman being given Her freedom. Imagine him telling his donkey, "Now, on The Sabbath you are not allowed to drink water, and on The Sabbath you must remain tied up to your post all day." That's basically what he was saying to this disabled Woman. He actually quotes several passages of SCRIPTURE about Shabbat when he says, "There are six days in which work ought to be done." But in the way he misinterpreted and misapplied those SCRIPTURE passages, he actually ends up completely opposing the very reason why Shabbat was given in the first place. That's why he was called a hypocrite.

If You ever wanted to leave a bad taste in someone's mouth concerning Shabbat, that would be the way to do it. If everyone kept Shabbat the way he did, we would only be left with one thing. Legalism. This ruler of The Synagogue forgot that Shabbat is not only for him but is for everyone else also. Instead of being so concerned with his own appearance and status quo, he should have rejoiced to see this Woman healed. He should have been more concerned with bringing freedom to others.

Let's translate this scenario into a more modern one. Let's say that you are an employer and have so many people under your employment. If you discover Shabbat in SCRIPTURE and begin to tell everyone about it and how you are now keeping it, be careful that it doesn't turn into being all about your appearance and reputation as a newly made Holy man just because you now keep The Sabbath. If your employees who also keep Shabbat come to you and ask that they also be able to take off work on Shabbat and you refuse them, you would absolutely be in hypocrisy. Your first thought in that scenario should be to give to others what you have been given, especially because they are under your employment and your responsibility. If that isn't your first thought, but instead you were hesitant to grant their request, that would be an obvious indication of two things:

- That you cared more about the revenue generated from them working on Shabbat than you do about what GOD says about them being given rest on HIS Holy Day.

- That your keeping of Shabbat was more of an outward show than an inward Fear and Love for THE LORD and Reverence for HIS Holy Day.

1. Are you setting THE LORD as your highest priority, or are there other things before HIM in your life?

   _____

   _____

   _____

2. What about all your other priorities—are they in order and lined up with THE WORD OF GOD?

   _____

   _____

   _____

3. When you gather before THE LORD (whether on the seventh day or the first day), what are you focused on, and what are you thinking about?

   _____

   _____

   _____

Additional Notes:

_____

_____

_____

_____

_____

_____

_____

Exodus 20:8-11
Exodus 23:9-12
Leviticus 19:30
Deuteronomy 5:12-15
Deuteronomy 6:4-9
Deuteronomy 11:18-20
Isaiah 58:6-14
Matthew 7:12
Mark 12:28-34
Luke 13:10-17

10.2 The Right Attitude and Priority

We can't possibly have the right attitude about THE LORD'S Sabbath if we don't even remember it. And that is exactly what we are instructed to do in Exodus 20:8. But how are we supposed to remember it? In what way should we think of Shabbat when we remember it?

Leviticus 19:30 says, "You shall keep my Sabbaths and reverence my sanctuary: I am THE LORD." Notice that The Sabbath and THE SANCTUARY are mentioned right next to one another in this verse. The two practically go hand in hand. Shabbat is The Day when we are to appear in GOD'S PRESENCE and meet with HIM. But it is not only HIS SANCTUARY that we should reverence. We should consider all the things of GOD in this way including The Day that HE set aside for us to meet with HIM in HIS SANCTUARY.

In the previous study we talked about the translations that different versions of SCRIPTURE use for Isaiah 58:13. As we mentioned in that study, most versions of SCRIPTURE will translate that verse as either "not talking idly" or "not speaking your own words" on Shabbat. But what exactly does that mean practically speaking? We have to remember and consider that The Sabbath is Holy because GOD HIMSELF made it so. It is unlike all the other weekdays, and so we should speak accordingly on Shabbat. In other words, don't spend your Shabbat talking about all the things you usually talk about. Don't spend your Shabbat talking about the things of this world, things that are carnal, or things of the flesh.

So, if we shouldn't talk about regular worldly things on Shabbat, what are we supposed to talk about, and how are we supposed to speak? There is a particular passage of SCRIPTURE that is absolutely foundational to anyone's walk with GOD. It is found first in Deuteronomy 6:4-9 and then repeated in Deuteronomy 11:18-20. It is called "The Sh'ma," and it is so important that, in Mark 12:28-30, YESHUA HIMSELF referred to this passage of SCRIPTURE as "The Greatest Commandment." And one of the instructions found in The Sh'ma in both of these passages from Deuteronomy is to speak of THE WORDS OF GOD "when you sit in your house, and when you walk by the way, and when you lie down, and when you rise up." So if we are already supposed to talk about THE WORD OF THE LORD this often, and Isaiah 58:13 tells us that we are not to "speak idly" or "speak your own words" on Shabbat, it should be simple enough to replace one with the other.

You may be asking, "Why are we focusing so much on what we talk about on Shabbat?" It's because everything you say flows directly from your heart, and the heart is what this chapter is all about. What it really comes down to is setting Shabbat in its rightful place in your priorities. If we love THE LORD and remember HIS Sabbath in reverence as we ought to, we will end up doing what is written in Isaiah 58:13-14. These two verses basically say to refrain from doing the things you want to do on Shabbat and still call The Day a "delight" and "honorable." It is impossible to think about Shabbat in this way and still be wondering what time the service will be over, what your profits look like at that moment, or what time the game starts.

So that's how we are supposed to consider Shabbat just for ourselves. But what about when it comes to other people? There are at least three SCRIPTURE passages that can help to answer that question. Exodus 20:8-11, Exodus 23:9-12, and Deuteronomy 5:12-15 make mention of keeping Shabbat specifically for the sake of those who belong to you. These passages clearly indicate that when you keep Shabbat, it is not only for you but also for your Son, your Daughter, your male servant, your female servant, the son of your female servant, the sojourner within your gates, and even your livestock. All these different types of people are mentioned throughout these passages because THE LORD cares for them and wants them to have rest on The Sabbath also. And if HE expects those who belong to you to have rest as well as you, that means HE expects you to make sure they get that rest.

All three of these passages say very similar things, but there are important differences between them. In order to accurately illustrate those differences, we could paraphrase them like this:

- Exodus 20:8-11 basically says, "You and they shall rest." (instruction)

- Exodus 23:9-12 basically says, "You shall rest so that they may rest." (instruction and reason)

- Deuteronomy 5:12-15 basically says, "You shall rest so that they may rest. And here's why you should want them to have rest." (instruction, reason, and motivation)

Because of this motivation, Deuteronomy 5:14-15 is really the best example of what our attitude toward other people concerning Shabbat should be. Essentially, Deuteronomy 5:14-15 says, "Give rest to your whole house and remember how THE LORD freed you from your slavery in Egypt." In other words, the memory of their freedom from Egypt was the very reason why they should have wanted to give freedom to others on Shabbat. This is one of the best and earliest BIBLICAL examples of how Matthew 7:12 should have been implemented. It is also the exact opposite of what the hypocrite in Luke 13:10-17 was doing. If he had adopted the mindset described in Deuteronomy 5:14-15, he wouldn't have fallen into such hypocrisy.

1. What a person fills their heart with will eventually come out in one way or another. What have you filled your heart with?

    _____

    _____

    _____

2. What is your motivation on Shabbat? Do you consider how you could give rest to others?

    _____

    _____

    _____

3. In light of this whole chapter, does your outer appearance match up with your inward reality?

    _____

    _____

    _____

Additional Notes:

_____

_____

_____

_____

_____

_____

_____

CHAPTER 11

What Is Shabbat Really About?

Genesis 1:1-31
Dominion over everything that moves on The Earth.

Genesis 2:1-3
The only Day of the week with no beginning and no end.

Exodus 20:8-11
Everyone Gets To Rest. A Day Blessed By GOD.
A Commemoration Of Creation.

Exodus 23:9-12
Everyone Gets To Rest.

Exodus 31:12-17
A Sign And A Covenant Between GOD And You.
A Commemoration Of Creation.

Leviticus 16:29-31
Yom Kippur/The Day of Atonement is the only Mo'edim
that is called a Shabbat.

Leviticus 24:1-9
The Bread of THE PRESENCE arranged every Shabbat.
A Covenant forever.

Leviticus 25:1-55
The year of release, redemption, and THE LORD'S favor.

Numbers 28:1-10
The Grain Offering on Shabbat is double the regular amount.

Deuteronomy 5:12-15
Everyone Gets To Rest.
A Day that commemorates The Freedom from slavery.

Deuteronomy 15:1-5
Freedom and release from all debts in the seventh year.

Deuteronomy 15:12-15
All the slaves go free in the seventh year.

Deuteronomy 24:17-22
An extra portion for all The People.

1 Kings 5:3-5
Phase two – THE KINGDOM is established
with Peace on every side.

2 Kings 4:18-23
Shabbat is the usual time to meet with GOD.

2 Kings 11:1-12:15
A 7-year-old King coronated on the seventh Day while
guarded by the first and last priests.

1 Chronicles 28:1-7
Phase one – A Man Of War And Blood.

2 Chronicles 22:10-24:14
A 7-year-old King coronated on the seventh day while
guarded by the first and last priests.

Nehemiah 13:15-22
Jerusalem's City gates closed for business on Shabbat.

Psalm 51:15-17
The right kind of Sacrifice.

Psalm 92:1-15
A Psalm for The Sabbath.

Isaiah 46:9-10
THE LORD declares the end from the beginning.

Isaiah 55:1-3
Come and buy without price.

Isaiah 58:6-14
How YESHUA kept Shabbat.
The reward for HIS kings.

Isaiah 61:1-3
How YESHUA kept Shabbat.

Ezekiel 46:1-5
The inner gate leading into GOD'S PRESENCE
is only open on Shabbat.

Matthew 11:27-12:14
How YESHUA kept Shabbat.
He breaks the yoke of slavery and gives us HIS Yoke.

Mark 1:21-31
YESHUA taught SCRIPTURE.

Mark 2:23-3:6
How YESHUA kept Shabbat.
A Day to save life and to heal.

Mark 6:1-2
YESHUA taught SCRIPTURE.

Luke 4:14-22
How YESHUA kept Shabbat.
YESHUA taught SCRIPTURE.

Luke 4:31-39
YESHUA taught SCRIP TURE.
He breaks the yoke of slavery and gives us HIS Yoke.

Luke 6:1-11
How YESHUA kept Shabbat.
He breaks the yoke of slavery and gives us HIS Yoke.

Luke 7:18-23
How YESHUA kept Shabbat.
He breaks the yoke of slavery and gives us HIS Yoke.

Luke 10:38-42
Put down your anxiety and focus on YESHUA.

Luke 13:10-17
How YESHUA kept Shabbat.
He breaks the yoke of slavery and gives us HIS Yoke.

Luke 14:1-24
How YESHUA kept Shabbat.
He breaks the yoke of slavery and gives us HIS Yoke.

John 1:29
THE BLOOD OF THE LAMB is your right of entry into HIS Rest.

John 5:5-18
How YESHUA kept Shabbat.
He breaks the yoke of slavery and gives us HIS Yoke.

John 6:22-68
HE will not reject anyone who comes to HIM.

John 7:14-24
How YESHUA kept Shabbat.
He breaks the yoke of slavery and gives us HIS Yoke.

John 9:1-16
How YESHUA kept Shabbat.
He breaks the yoke of slavery and gives us HIS Yoke.

John 10:7-11
HE IS THE DOOR to abundant Life.

Acts 16:13
A Day to bring an offering to GOD and come into HIS PRESENCE.

Romans 12:1-2
Think like a living sacrifice so You can be a living sacrifice.

1 Corinthians 15:45-47
YESHUA is called "THE LAST ADAM."

2 Corinthians 3:16-18
There is freedom in THE PRESENCE OF THE LORD.

Colossians 2:13-17
A shadow of things to come.

Hebrews 3:7-4:11
Entering into THE LORD'S rest.

1 John 4:19
Shabbat is a love gift from THE LORD.
Now it's our turn.

Revelation 21:22-25
No more evening, night, or morning.
Only eternal Day.

Revelation 22:3-5
No more evening, night, or morning.
Only eternal Day.

Introduction to Chapter 11
You May Have Seen These Before

In chapter 7, we established clearly that YESHUA did in
fact keep Shabbat. But we did not fully discuss how HE kept
Shabbat. Several things introduced in previous chapters will be
brought back up in this chapter. That is because in this chapter,
we're going to try to bring all those things together. This will
be not only for the purpose of showing you how YESHUA kept
Shabbat, but also to bring out the deeper meanings of The
Sabbath and what it represents. So, let's dive in and see if we can
find what Shabbat is really all about.

Genesis 1:1-31
Mark 1:21-31
Mark 6:1-2
Luke 4:14-22
Luke 4:31-39
Luke 13:10-17
Luke 14:1-24
1 Corinthians 15:45-47

11.1 How Did YESHUA Keep The Sabbath? Part 1 HE Spoke and Taught THE WORD OF GOD in the Synagogues

Every one of these passages from THE GOSPELS except for
Luke 14:1-24 mention that it was YESHUA'S practice to teach in
the Synagogues on Shabbat. In Luke 14:1-24 HE also taught The
People while seated at a dinner table at a pharisee's house on
Shabbat. And HE wasn't just teaching them language or history
either. HE was teaching them THE WORD OF GOD. One
example of this is in Luke 4:16-21 when HE taught them from
the Scroll of Isaiah The Prophet.

And YESHUA was not merely teaching SCRIPTURE the same
way anyone else would. Mark 1:21-22, Mark 6:1-2, and Luke
4:31-32 say that HIS teaching was "astonishing." But how was
it "astonishing" and what made it so? Two things: Power and
Authority.

Power has to do with strength and ability. Luke 4:36 speaks about
YESHUA in this way. "What is this word? For with authority and
"*Power*" HE commands the unclean spirits, and they come out!"
But where did HE get this Power? We find the source of HIS
Power a few verses earlier in the same chapter. Luke 4:14 says,
"JESUS returned in The Power of THE SPIRIT."

Authority has to do with position, rank, or status. It says in
both Mark 1:21-27 and Luke 4:31-36 that YESHUA'S Words

and teaching held "*Authority*." All the way back in Genesis 1:28, GOD gave Adam dominion over everything that moves on Earth. In 1 Corinthians 15:45-47, YESHUA is called "THE LAST ADAM." And many times in The Gospels, HE calls HIMSELF "THE SON OF MAN." And because HE lived a sinless life, HE had every right to take up and use the authority and dominion that was originally given to The First Adam before the fall.

It is with this kind of Power and Authority that YESHUA spoke THE WORDS OF GOD and taught SCRIPTURE to The People on Shabbat, even to the point of telling them that a particular SCRIPTURE was fulfilled in HIM as HE did in Luke 4:18-21. By doing this, HE truly spoke Life to The People on The Sabbath. That is why HE is the very reason for our convocation. It is specifically for the purpose of hearing what HE would speak.

1.   If YESHUA was not recognizable and HE came into most Churches speaking this way, would HE be accepted? Would you accept HIM?

_____

_____

_____

2.   What if you could sit at YESHUA'S Feet and learn from HIM while HE was speaking this way for just one day?

_____

_____

_____

3.   Have you ever considered seeking THE LORD for more Power and Grace to overcome a particular situation or sin?

_____

_____

_____

Additional Notes:

_____

_____

_____

_____

_____

_____

Matthew 11:27-12:14
Mark 1:21-31
Mark 2:23-3:6
Luke 4:31-39
Luke 6:1-11
Luke 13:10-17
Luke 14:1-24
John 5:5-18
John 9:1-16

11.2 How Did YESHUA keep The Sabbath? Part 2 HE Healed Them and Set Them Free

So, YESHUA spoke words of Life in Power and Authority to The People on Shabbat. But what did HE do with these words of Power and Authority? How did HE use them?

Matthew 12:9-14, Mark 3:1-6, and Luke 6:6-11 all contain different accounts of the same event—that of YESHUA healing the man with a withered hand on Shabbat. Healing people is one thing that HE did repeatedly on The Sabbath. In Luke 13:10-13 YESHUA heals the woman who was bent over and could not straighten her back, and in Luke 14:1-4, HE heals a man from dropsy. In John 5:5-9 YESHUA heals a man who was lame and could not walk for 38 years, and in John 9:1-7 HE heals a man who had been blind from birth. Every single one of these healings was done by YESHUA on The Sabbath. Take special note of these last two passages in anticipation of part 5 of this series of studies called "How Did YESHUA Keep The Sabbath?" When you consider these two passages of SCRIPTURE, remember this phrase, "The lame walk, and the blind see."

There is one more instance of YESHUA healing on Shabbat that is a very peculiar case—that of YESHUA healing Simon's Mother-in-law of a fever. This event is covered in both Mark 1:29-31 and Luke 4:38-39. The reason why this healing is so peculiar is because you can come away with a slightly different impression of it depending on which GOSPEL you are reading. In Mark's GOSPEL, it doesn't really appear to be any different than any of the other healings that YESHUA performed. But in Luke's GOSPEL, it specifically says that HE "rebuked the fever." That seems odd, doesn't it? In most of the other healings that YESHUA performed whether on The Sabbath or not, it doesn't say that HE rebuked the sickness. HE would usually just heal the sickness. But you know what HE did rebuke on a constant basis? demons.

Many times in THE GOSPELS when YESHUA was healing people, HE was also rebuking and casting out demons. So much so that HIS healing ministry and HIS deliverance ministry were just about inseparable. And there are several cases when HE healed someone of a sickness or infirmity specifically by casting out the demon that was causing the sickness or infirmity. This could easily become an entirely separate teaching by itself. But for right now, suffice it to say that this was also the case for some of the healings that YESHUA performed on Shabbat. Let's take a look at a few of those now.

I believe the passages we discussed earlier fit into this category. In Luke 4:38-39 YESHUA heals Simon's Mother-in-law of a fever specifically by rebuking it. You don't rebuke something that isn't able to hear and receive the rebuke. I believe that is evidence enough to say that this fever was demonically influenced and that YESHUA was actually rebuking and casting out a demon that was causing the fever. Maybe you're not convinced. Maybe you're saying something like, "I don't think there's quite enough in the text to be able to prove that theory." Fair enough. But the same cannot be said about this next example.

In Luke 13:10-17 YESHUA heals a Woman who is bent over and cannot straighten her back; verses 16 and 11 tell us exactly what was causing this condition. Verse 16 says, "a daughter of Abraham whom *satan* bound" and verse 11 says "a woman who had a *disabling spirit*." Some versions of SCRIPTURE will use this phrase "disabling spirit," and other versions will use the phrase "spirit of infirmity." But the point here is that her disability was directly caused by a spirit sent from the enemy.

And that's not the only time YESHUA had to deal with a demon on Shabbat. In both Mark 1:21-28 and Luke 4:31-37, HE is casting an unclean spirit out of a man in The Synagogue on Shabbat. Notice that the demon did not manifest until YESHUA began teaching; it seemed to be perfectly comfortable in The Church or Synagogue until THE PRESENCE OF GOD entered in. This is what Shabbat is really all about. Because when you enter into THE PRESENCE OF THE LORD, all evil and darkness along with the cares of this world have to flee away; those things can do nothing except flee away when HE is there. And it was when YESHUA cast out this demon that The People recognized that HIS WORD and Teaching had The Power and Authority we discussed earlier.

Now, we come back to the original question we started this study with: What did YESHUA do with these Words of Power and Authority? HE spoke Life to The People in order to set them free from their bondages and oppressions on Shabbat whether they were purely medical or demonically influenced. HE spoke THE WORD to them in order to break their yokes off their backs.

1. Have you ever noticed that everything seems to be going just fine until you start getting ready for and heading to Church or Synagogue and then you begin to be attacked and harassed by every circumstance?

_____

_____

_____

2. Have you ever considered that it is no coincidence? Have you ever tried rebuking it in THE NAME OF JESUS?

_____

_____

_____

3. What kind of bondages do you need THE LORD to set YOU free from in your life so that you can have rest?

_____

_____

_____

Additional Notes:

_____

_____

_____

_____

_____

_____

Exodus 20:8-11
Exodus 23:9-12
Deuteronomy 5:12-15
Matthew 11:27-12:14
John 6:22-68

11.3 How Did YESHUA Keep The Sabbath? Part 3 HE Gave Rest to All and Never Turned Anyone Away

There is a recurring theme running through these first three passages that can be summed up by saying, "Shabbat is not only for you. It is not only for the important or rich people. GOD gave The Sabbath to all HIS People, so make sure everyone gets to enjoy a Sabbath rest." In Exodus 20:8-11, Exodus 23:9-12, and Deuteronomy 5:12-15, there are several categories of people and animals specifically mentioned that should also be given rest. Those categories include sons, daughters, male servants, female servants, the sons of female servants, sojourners, resident aliens, and even oxen and donkeys. That doesn't really leave anyone out.

And that is exactly how YESHUA kept Shabbat as well. We can see this all throughout HIS ministry but especially in John 6:35-37. In these verses, HE gives three different promises, and each one starts with the word "whoever." Those promises are:

- "whoever comes to me shall not hunger"
- "whoever comes to me shall never thirst"
- "whoever comes to me I will never cast out"

Perhaps one of the most encouraging Promises of GOD in all of SCRIPTURE is in Matthew 11:27-30, and it too is written to all who would come. In this passage YESHUA says:

"²⁷ All things have been handed over to me by My FATHER, and no one knows THE SON except THE FATHER, and no one knows THE FATHER except THE SON and *anyone* to whom THE SON chooses to reveal him. ²⁸ Come to me, *all* who labor and are heavy laden, and I will give you rest. ²⁹ Take my yoke upon you, and learn from me, for I am gentle and lowly in heart, and you will find rest for your souls. For my yoke is easy, and my burden is light."

This is what Shabbat is really about—not only finding rest for your body but finding rest for your Soul as well. And that rest is only found in YESHUA. What a blessed gift it is that HE has made available to all who would come to HIM—that we would be able to set down our burdens and take up HIS yoke instead and find rest for our souls.

Whether HE was in The Synagogue or on the streets. Whether HE was ministering in Teaching, Healing, Deliverance, or a combination of the three. Whether the people were Jew, Gentile, or pagan. Whether the bondages and oppressions The People bore were spiritual, mental, physical, medical, or demonically influenced, YESHUA never turned anyone away. HE gave peace, rest, and healing to whoever came to HIM. In each and every one of these scenarios, YESHUA did the same thing: HE spoke Life to them in order to set them free from their bondages and oppressions no matter who they were.

1. Can you think of any ways that you could give rest to someone in your life?

_____

_____

_____

2. Have you ever unjustly turned anyone away before? How could you make that right?

_____

_____

_____

3. Is there any particular area of your life in which you are trying to carry your own burden instead of YESHUA'S burden?

_____

_____

_____

Additional Notes:

_____

_____

_____

_____

_____

_____

_____

Matthew 11:27-12:14
Mark 2:23-3:6
Luke 6:1-11
Luke 13:10-17
Luke 14:1-24
John 7:14-24

11.4 How Did YESHUA Keep The Sabbath? Part 4 The Mind Of MESSIAH

So far we've talked about how YESHUA spoke THE WORD OF GOD and spoke life in Power and Authority to The People on Shabbat. We learned that HE used that Power and Authority to heal people and set them free from bondage and oppression and that HE didn't refuse or turn away anyone who came to HIM for these things. These are all the things that YESHUA regularly did on Shabbat, and this is how HE kept Shabbat.

Now, the question is . . . What was HE thinking? No, I mean that literally. What was HE thinking that made HIM keep Shabbat in this way? How did THE MESSIAH think about The Sabbath so that this was HIS interpretation of how Shabbat should be kept? Have you ever wondered what YESHUA thought about this SCRIPTURE or that one? Or what HIS theology was? I don't know about you, but if I discovered the way THE MESSIAH HIMSELF believed about a certain thing, I wouldn't so much consider it to be HIS opinion as I would consider it to be BIBLICAL fact. If we look carefully through some of THE GOSPEL accounts, there are several things that YESHUA says to indicate exactly what HE believed about Shabbat, how HE thought about Shabbat, and why HE considered that it should be kept in this way. It is those passages that we will be examining in this study.

In both Matthew 12:9-10 and Luke 14:2-3, the question is asked: "Is it lawful to heal on The Sabbath, or not?" And in both accounts, YESHUA responds to that question by healing on

The Sabbath. So, we can know based on these two SCRIPTURE passages that YESHUA believed that it absolutely "is lawful to do good on The Sabbath" and that it is lawful to heal someone on Shabbat according to HIS own actions. But again, what were HIS Thoughts or HIS Motivations that brought HIM to such a conclusion about The Sabbath?

In Luke 13:15-16 we find YESHUA'S response to the hypocritical error of the ruler of the Synagogue concerning this Woman with a disabling spirit. Examining the kind of language YESHUA uses while rebuking him will be very helpful in our understanding of why THE SON OF GOD kept The Sabbath the way HE did. For that purpose, let's examine those two verses in their entirety:

> "15 You hypocrites! Does not each of you on The Sabbath *untie* his ox or his donkey from the manger and lead it away to water it? 16And ought not this woman, a daughter of Abraham whom satan has *bound* for eighteen years, be *loosed* from this *bond* on The Sabbath Day?"

Do you notice the freedom versus slavery kind of language YESHUA is using here? It is necessary to understand that in this passage, HE is not only calling out the hypocrisy in this man's priorities but YESHUA is also comparing the way he is treating this Woman to the treatment he gives to his ox or donkey. This man was willing to give his own ox or donkey rest and freedom by untying it from where it was bound. But he was unwilling that a Daughter of Abraham would receive Her freedom on the same Day even though GOD HIMSELF cares much more for people than for an ox or a donkey.

This passage of SCRIPTURE is one of several places where YESHUA makes this kind of comparison between people and their animals concerning Shabbat. Matthew 12:11-12 and Luke 14:5 are two more examples of this kind of comparison. These two passages of SCRIPTURE basically say the same thing. If you were to summarize the two, it would probably be something like this: "The good you are willing to do for your animals on Shabbat, you definitely ought to be willing to do for people as well."

YESHUA HIMSELF says in Matthew 12:12, "Of how much more value is a man than a sheep!" This quote could appear as if HE is asking them about the value of men and sheep, but notice that this quote does not end with a question mark. It ends with an exclamation mark. In other words, HE is not asking them; HE is telling them that a man is of much more value.

Now let's take another quick look at Luke 13:15. Where is the ox or donkey untied from? From a manger. What is a manger like? It's a place where animals are kept and therefore a place where animal excrement would constantly be present. The point is that it would not be a clean place. This unclean place can be compared to a person's life of sin. Therefore if on Shabbat an ox or donkey is untied from a manger and led away to water, how much more should The Sabbath be a Day when GOD'S Own Children are set free from their sin and led into GOD'S PRESENCE where they can drink freely of THE LIVING WATER? And if on The Sabbath it is good for someone to exert the effort it takes to lift up their sheep out of a pit (Matthew 12:11), then how much more should Shabbat be a Day when the precious souls of GOD'S Own Children are lifted up and saved from the pit of hell?

Shabbat is about life and peace, freedom and healing. John 7:22-24 is another excellent example of this. In verse 23 of this passage, YESHUA says, "If on The Sabbath a man receives circumcision, so that The Law of Moses may not be broken, are you angry with me because on The Sabbath I made a man's whole body well?" The obvious implication of this is that it was incredibly ridiculous and unreasonable for them to be angry about such a thing because Shabbat is The Day when these sorts of things ought to be done.

In both Mark 3:4 and Luke 6:9, YESHUA asks the same very intentional question: "Is it lawful on The Sabbath to do good or to do harm, to save life or to kill?" HIS actions all over HIS earthly ministry gave the answer to that question. But if that wasn't enough, HE also gave us the answer outright in Matthew 12:12. It is clear from all this that THE MESSIAH HIMSELF saw The Sabbath as a Day to give, preserve, and save life.

1. How does YESHUA'S perspective of The Sabbath affect what you may have previously understood about Shabbat?

_____

_____

_____

2. Is there anything specific that you could learn from YESHUA'S perspective of Shabbat?

_____

_____

_____

3. Can you think of any ways that you could implement these things in your own life?

_____

_____

_____

Additional Notes:

_____

_____

_____

_____

_____

_____

_____

Leviticus 25:1-55
Deuteronomy 15:1-5
Deuteronomy 15:12-15
Isaiah 58:6-14
Isaiah 61:1-3
Matthew 11:27-12:14
Luke 4:14-22
Luke 7:18-23
John 10:7-11

11.5 How Did YESHUA Keep The Sabbath? Part 5 What Messiah Came to Do

Let's begin this last study on how YESHUA kept Shabbat with a quick recap of what we have discussed so far in the previous studies:

- Part 1 – HE spoke THE WORD OF GOD and life to The People in Power and Authority.

- Part 2 – HE set The People free from their sins, oppressions, infirmities, and demons.

- Part 3 – HE never turned anyone away, and HE gave peace, rest, freedom, and healing to whoever came to HIM.

- Part 4 – HE saw The Sabbath as a time to give, preserve, and save life.

These could be the main points to take away from the previous four studies. The reason why this recap is important is that this study is intended to be compared to everything we've already learned in these four previous studies.

This study really has to begin with Luke 4:14-22 because of the claim that YESHUA makes at the end of this passage. In this passage and particularly in verse 21, YESHUA says that THE

SCRIPTURE that HE had just quoted was "fulfilled in your hearing." Now we have to find out what SCRIPTURE HE was reading from so that we can know what YESHUA meant when HE said it was "fulfilled in your hearing." HE was reading directly from Isaiah 61:1-3.

You will notice a few things about these two passages. First, the things that are listed in these passages are exactly the things that YESHUA did in HIS earthly ministry and especially on Shabbat. Second, both of these passages make specific mention of something called "the favorable year of THE LORD" or "the year of THE LORD'S Favor." So, what is this time that is quoted by YESHUA, and what is its meaning? The time called "the favorable year of THE LORD" is also referred to in SCRIPTURE as "the year of release," and this time takes place every *seven* years.

There are at least two whole chapters in THE TORAH that are completely devoted to this time. One of those chapters is Leviticus 25, and the other is Deuteronomy 15. Both of these chapters go into different levels of detail about exactly what is supposed to happen every *seven* years on the year of release. So, when YESHUA says it is "fulfilled in your hearing," HE is not only saying that about Isaiah 61:1-3 but also about Leviticus 25 and Deuteronomy 15 and every prophetic prediction made from those two chapters of TORAH concerning this time. HE is basically saying that HIS ministry fulfills all of those things, so let's find out what some of them are.

In Leviticus 25:1-7 we find that the *seventh* year is to be a Sabbath rest for The Land. This would mean that no farming, tilling, or reaping would be done in any way to The Land during this entire year. And even though there would be no reaping during this time, verses 6-7 say that The Land will provide enough food for everyone. So again, we find another situation where THE LORD gives an extra Blessing of added provisions for obeying HIS WORD concerning this Sabbath year for The Land. And so far we have already identified at least two things from these verses that can be related back to YESHUA's ministry:

1. The whole land gets a rest for a whole year.
2. An extra blessing of provision from GOD through The Land. (A quick side note: Item 2 makes The Disciples plucking grain on Shabbat and YESHUA cursing the fig tree make so much more sense because it was the year for those things to happen.)

In Deuteronomy 15 we find at least two more things that tie right back into what we were discussing in part 2 of this series titled "HE Healed Them and Set Them Free." The first one is in Deuteronomy 15:1-5. SCRIPTURE says in this passage that every debt is to be forgiven in The Year of Release. What is the one thing that gives oppression a legal right to be there? It's debt. If You owe money or something else to either an individual or an organization, they have a legal right to oppress you and make you work it off or pay it off. But where there is no debt, there can be no oppression.

And that is probably the most well-known thing about YESHUA and what HE came to do. HE came to pay the price for our sins, thereby achieving forgiveness of our debts to GOD. But there are also several places throughout THE GOSPELS where HE forgave someone their sins well before HE went to THE CROSS. So now we have #3.

3. All debts are forgiven.

And the second one that is found in Deuteronomy 15 is in verses 12-15. We can see from these verses that this *seventh* year is also the time when all those who are enslaved and held captive are to be set free. Doesn't that sound exactly like what YESHUA did by setting them free from their demonic enslavers? And there we have #4.

4. Freedom to the captives.

So by a careful reading through the verses in Leviticus 25:1-7, Deuteronomy 15:1-5, and Deuteronomy 15:12-15, we've come away with at least four things that are entirely relevant to both "the favorable year of THE LORD" and YESHUA'S ministry which is a fulfillment of it. Those four things are:

1. The whole land gets a rest for a whole year.
2. An extra blessing of provision from GOD through The Land.
3. All debts are forgiven.
4. Freedom to the captives.

It is important to remember that the two TORAH chapters we just reviewed are what is being referenced by Isaiah 61:1-3, which is the portion of SCRIPTURE that YESHUA said was fulfilled by HIS ministry on The Sabbath. Now in order for that claim to be true (and it is), there are some very specific things that YESHUA would have to do during HIS earthly ministry. Isaiah 61:1-3 would require a very specific job description from YESHUA. If you take a moment to read this passage of SCRIPTURE, you will find that job description looks something like this:

Bring good news to the poor.
Bind up the broken-hearted.
Proclaim liberty to the captives.
Proclaim the opening of the prison to those who are bound.
Proclaim the year of THE LORD's Favor.
Proclaim the day of vengeance of GOD.
Comfort all who mourn in Zion.

If you include the four things that were gleaned from Leviticus 25 and Deuteronomy 15, that's already quite a lot that YESHUA said was directly fulfilled by HIS ministry. But there a few other verses I believe are also a very good description of how YESHUA kept Shabbat even though HE may not have made the same claim of fulfillment for them as HE did with the other verses. Two such portions of SCRIPTURE would be Isaiah 58:6-14 and Luke 7:18-23 from which we can see very similar job descriptions to what we found in Isaiah 61:1-3. So, what if we break down those two portions of SCRIPTURE the way we broke down Isaiah 61:1-3 and then added in all the other things that YESHUA did on Shabbat? Then you would be left with something like this:

Leviticus 25:1-7, Deuteronomy 15:1-5, Deuteronomy 15:12-15

1. The whole land gets a rest for a whole year.
2. An extra blessing of provision from GOD through The Land.
3. All debts are forgiven.
4. Freedom to the captives.

Isaiah 58:6-14

Loose the bonds of wickedness.
Undo the straps of the yoke.
Let the oppressed go free.
Break every yoke.
Share your bread with the hungry.
Bring the homeless poor into your house.
Clothe the naked.
Don't hide yourself from your own flesh.
Take away the yoke from your midst.
Take away finger-pointing and speaking wickedness.
Pour yourself out for the hungry.
Satisfy the desire of the afflicted.

Isaiah 61:1-3

Bring good news to the poor.
Bind up the broken-hearted.
Proclaim liberty to the captives.
Proclaim the opening of the prison to those who are bound.
Proclaim the year of THE LORD's Favor.
Proclaim the day of vengeance of GOD.
Comfort all who mourn in Zion.

Luke 7:18-23

The blind receive their sight.
The lame walk.
Lepers are cleansed.
The deaf hear.
The dead are raised up.
The poor have good news preached to them.

Parts 1-4 of this chapter:

Part 1 – HE spoke THE WORD OF GOD and life to The People in Power and Authority.

Part 2 – HE set The People free from their sins, oppressions, infirmities, and demons.

Part 3 – HE never turned anyone away, but HE gave peace, rest, freedom, and healing to whoever came to HIM.

Part 4 – HE saw Shabbat as a time to give, preserve, and save life.

That is one impressive resume. Especially when you consider that in some way or another, YESHUA fulfilled every one of these things on Shabbat during HIS earthly ministry. These are all the things that HE did on The Sabbath, and this is how HE kept The Sabbath. YESHUA says very clearly in Matthew 11:27-30 that HE gives us rest for our souls and that HE gives us life more abundantly according to John 10:10. Looking through this kind of resume, it's easy to see that's exactly what HE did. It is no wonder why HE is called "THE LORD Of The Sabbath."

1. After reading this study and in your own words, what would you say MESSIAH came to do?

_____

_____

_____

2. Does seeing HIS job description in this way help you appreciate or bring into perspective why only HE could be our MESSIAH and Atonement?

_____

_____

_____

3. Can you now see the correlation between The Sabbath and THE MESSIAH'S mission here on Earth? If so, how would you say that THE MESSIAH is revealed in The Sabbath?

_____

_____

_____

Additional Notes:

_____

_____

_____

_____

_____

_____

_____

Leviticus 24:1-9
Numbers 28:1-10
Deuteronomy 24:17-22
2 Kings 4:18-23
Psalm 51:15-17
Psalm 92:1-15
Matthew 11:27-12:14
Mark 2:23-3:6
Luke 6:1-11
Luke 10:38-42
Acts 16:13
Romans 12:1-2
1 John 4:19

11.6 Come and Bring Your Offering to the Altar

Clearly, 1 John 4:19 is especially true when it comes to Shabbat. "We love HIM because HE first loved us." But how? In what way are we to show our love for HIM? One way we can show it is in our gifts and offerings. As we have mentioned earlier, it is plain to see in 2 Kings 4:18-23 that Shabbat is definitely the time to appear before THE KING to bring such gifts and offerings. And this is not the only verse to make such a suggestion, especially when it comes to the grain offerings.

In Leviticus 24:5-9, The Bread Of THE PRESENCE was arranged on The Table of Showbread by The High Priest every Sabbath. And in Numbers 28:1-10, especially verses 5 and 9, we see that the grain offering was to be doubled on Shabbat. Because of this, Shabbat is also to be considered as "The Day of an extra provision" or "The Day of a double portion."

And this concept is played out in verses like Deuteronomy 24:17-22, Matthew 12:1-8, Mark 2:23-28, and Luke 6:1-5. In these three GOSPEL passages, The Disciples are passing through the *grain* fields, plucking heads of *grain* and eating them. Both of the SCRIPTURE passages in the previous paragraph are concerning the *grain* offering. So, not only is Shabbat The Day when we ought to show up with an extra offering to give to THE KING, but it is also The Day when THE KING HIMSELF provides for us an extra portion from THE BREAD OF LIFE. It is The Day set aside for a Holy exchange between THE KING and HIS People. We bring to HIM an extra portion of our offerings, our love, and our worship, and HE gives to us an extra portion of Life and Blessing.

But what kind of offering are we supposed bring to THE KING on Shabbat? Are we supposed to bring animals or food to HIM and HIS Priests as in ancient times? Maybe someday when a new TEMPLE is built, but for today those are not the kinds of offerings we are talking about. Psalm 92 is called "a Psalm for The Sabbath." And after reading the first five verses, it becomes incredibly obvious why it is called that. Psalm 92:1-5 is chocked full of the kinds of offerings that we are supposed to present to THE KING on Shabbat. Acts 16:13 is another great example of the kinds of offerings we should bring because The Apostle Paul and those with Him were looking for a place of Prayer on Shabbat. Between these two passages, there are all kinds of Prayers, Thanksgivings, Praises, Declarations, and Songs. That's a lot of offerings. But even these kinds of offerings can be made in a way that is unacceptable if they are offered hypocritically.

Psalm 51:15-17 makes it very clear not only that the heart and the attitude with which you bring your offerings is important, but also that your heart itself is the offering. If you have "a broken spirit and a contrite heart," you are the offering. Again, this is exactly what The Apostle Paul was referring to in Romans 12:1-2. I believe Luke 10:38-42 is also an excellent example of this concept. Martha is like the sacrifice of food, animals, and burnt offerings while Mary is like the sacrifice of Psalm 51:17. Martha tried the best She could to find an animal of sacrifice and make it spotless but failed. While Mary humbled Herself and made Herself the offering. Martha put Her service on The Altar but Mary put Herself on The Altar. I will ask You again: Will you be like Martha or Mary? What kind of sacrifice will you bring on Shabbat?

1. When you bring your offering to THE LORD, are you Worshiping in Spirit and Truth or in the flesh?

_____

_____

_____

2. Is there a particular area of your life where you would like to receive a double portion of THE BREAD OF LIFE from THE LORD?

_____

_____

_____

3. Is there any part of yourself that you know you need to put on The Altar?

_____

_____

_____

Additional Notes:

_____

_____

_____

_____

_____

_____

_____

Leviticus 16:29-31
Nehemiah 13:15-22
Ezekiel 46:1-5
John 1:29
John 6:22-68
John 10:7-11
2 Corinthians 3:16-18
Hebrews 3:7-4:11

11.7 Enter into HIS PRESENCE

So, we've seen already the immense love that GOD showed to HIS People by sending HIS SON to them. And we've already seen that it would only be right for us to respond in love and with an offering. But what offering could possibly be good enough to bring before THE KING? That is one of the things we'll be discussing in this study.

Between The Books of Nehemiah and Ezekiel, we find a very interesting contrast concerning Shabbat. In Nehemiah 13:17-22, we read that Nehemiah called for the city gates to be closed only on Shabbat unlike the rest of the week when they were open. And in Ezekiel 46:1-5, THE LORD HIMSELF is saying that the gate of The Inner Court of HIS TEMPLE will be open only on Shabbat unlike the rest of the week when it will be closed. Do you realize exactly what that means? It means that The Sabbath is the one Day out of the whole week when the doors into the world are shut, and The Door into THE PRESENCE OF THE LORD is open. I believe this is one of the things that makes The Sabbath a Prophetic picture of HEAVEN ITSELF.

Shabbat is the one Day when THE LORD has opened THE DOOR for us to enter HIS Rest. And The Sabbath itself is a picture of GOD'S Eternal Rest for HIS People. Yet a careful reading of Hebrews 3:7-4:11 tells us very clearly that some have failed to enter HIS Rest because of unbelief. And if it was unbelief that kept them out, then it is belief in YESHUA that will grant you entry because YESHUA HIMSELF is THE DOOR into

GOD'S PRESENCE (John 10:7-11). Believe in HIM who is THE DOOR so that you may enter by THE DOOR.

But this DOOR doesn't open for you just because you want HIM to. There is a certain something that you must have in order that this DOOR may open for You. That is THE BLOOD OF THE LAMB OF GOD (John 1:29). It is worth noting that in Leviticus 16:29-31, The Day of Atonement is also called "a Sabbath of solemn rest." I believe this is because the events that The Day of Atonement is all about are the very reason why we are able to enter into THE LORD'S Eternal Sabbath in the first place. And this same passage says that The Day of Atonement is also a time to rest and to afflict oneself. Have you ever wondered why that is? It's because it is THE BLOOD that YESHUA shed through HIS affliction that makes the final Atonement for us and therefore, it is what allows us to enter HIS Rest—much like the very first Passover. Only the houses that had The Blood on the door were safe. And so YESHUA is both THE DOOR that leads into GOD'S PRESENCE and the only perfect SACRIFICE that grants you entry into that DOOR.

Those who try to enter by any other way are thieves and robbers. But all those who enter by THE DOOR will be safe, find rest for their souls, and never be cast out (John 6:37). According to 2 Corinthians 3:16-18, all those who enter in will experience true freedom, simply because THE LORD is there.

1. Have you received THE BLOOD OF THE LAMB OF GOD on the doorpost of your heart?

   _____

   _____

   _____

2. If so, how often do you enter through THE DOOR and into HIS PRESENCE?

   _____

   _____

   _____

3. If you have found that you are granted access to THE LORD'S PRESENCE through this DOOR and you know there is no other entry, how much time do you spend telling others about this DOOR?

   _____

   _____

   _____

Additional Notes:

_____

_____

_____

_____

_____

_____

Genesis 1:1-31
Genesis 2:1-3
Exodus 20:8-11
Exodus 31:12-17
Leviticus 25:1-55
Deuteronomy 5:12-15
Deuteronomy 15:1-5
Deuteronomy 15:12-15
1 Kings 5:3-5
2 Kings 11:1-12:15
1 Chronicles 28:1-7
2 Chronicles 22:10-24:14
Isaiah 46:9-10
Isaiah 55:1-3
Isaiah 61:1-3
Luke 4:14-22
Colossians 2:13-17
Hebrews 3:7-4:11
Revelation 21:22-25
Revelation 22:3-5

11.8 A Type and Shadow of Another Time

You may have noticed by now that the latter part of this chapter has been ordered according to the layout of THE TEMPLE. First, we discussed what happens at The Altar, what kinds of offerings we ought to bring as gifts to Our LORD on Shabbat, and that YESHUA is the only offering that will grant entry through THE DOOR/VEIL. Next we highlighted the fact that Shabbat is the time that GOD has set aside for us to enter into HIS PRESENCE and to meet with HIM and that YESHUA HIMSELF is THE DOOR/VEIL by which we can enter into THE PRESENCE OF GOD. But what will it be like when we finally enter through THE DOOR and into HIS PRESENCE? We can infer at least a few answers to that question based on some key SCRIPTURES. There are at least five different time periods that are directly compared to Shabbat by THE SCRIPTURES that refer to those time periods. In this last study of this chapter, we will be discussing those time periods and why SCRIPTURE makes this comparison to Shabbat.

The first two of these five time periods are found in THE TORAH. Three times in THE TORAH, THE LORD gives us reasons why we should keep Shabbat—twice in Exodus and once in Deuteronomy. In Exodus 20:8-11 GOD is giving The People of Israel practical ways to keep Shabbat, but specifically in verse 11, HE says the reason for keeping Shabbat in this way is because HE "made heaven and earth, the sea and all that is in them" in six days and rested on the seventh. In Exodus 31:12-17 HE says basically the same thing with a slight difference. The difference is that in verse 17, HE calls Shabbat a sign that HE "made heaven and earth and on the seventh day HE rested and was refreshed." By speaking about it this way, HE also made the institution of The Sabbath a memorial of Creation.

And Deuteronomy 5:12-15 is very similar to the first verse from Exodus. Only this time, the reason for keeping Shabbat is their memory of how THE LORD *freed* them from slavery in Egypt. This is what Shabbat is really all about—Freedom from your slavery. That means Freedom from slavery to physical or spiritual oppressions, freedom from slavery to sin, and freedom from slavery to the kingdom of this world. And so we have already covered two of the five time periods that Shabbat is compared to by SCRIPTURE. The first one is Creation and the second one is The Israelis' freedom from Egypt.

As we discussed earlier in this chapter, there are places in SCRIPTURE that refer to the time called "the favorable year of THE LORD," which is also called a year of Sabbath rest for The Land. These SCRIPTURES are Leviticus 25:1-55 and Deuteronomy 15:1-15. Isaiah 61:1-3 refers to and prophesies about this time in future tense by speaking about the one who would be sent to proclaim, "the favorable year of THE LORD."

And Isaiah 61:1-3 is the passage that YESHUA quotes in the Synagogue on The Sabbath in Luke 4:14-22 saying that it was "fulfilled in your hearing." So, the time that is also called a year of Sabbath rest for The Land is the time that YESHUA said was fulfilled by HIS earthly ministry on The Sabbath. This is very appropriate considering how many people received rest and relief specifically because of what HE did during HIS ministry. And so YESHUA'S earthly ministry is the third time period that SCRIPTURE directly compares to The Sabbath.

In Colossians 2:13-17 we find a very interesting statement about Shabbat and about the rest of the Holy Days. In verse 16 The Apostle Paul mentions things like Festivals, New Moons, and Sabbaths, and then He says this about those things in verse 17: "These are a shadow of things to come." This is especially true when it comes to Shabbat.

For example, if you compare each day of the week to a specific period of a thousand years in history, then Shabbat would be the seventh and last thousand-year period during which YESHUA HIMSELF will rule and reign over everything on Earth from HIS THRONE in Jerusalem. And there are several other places in SCRIPTURE that represent both Shabbat and The Millennial Reign of CHRIST together. Let's begin with a brief description of what will happen upon YESHUA'S return, HIS Millennial Reign, and the events leading up to it, so we can know exactly what we're comparing these SCRIPTURES to.

In the final days every nation will be against Israel and Jerusalem and will be waging war against Her. When YESHUA returns, HE will return exactly the same way HE ascended, and HE will return to exactly the same place HE ascended from. HE will touch down on and set HIS Feet on the Mount of Olives, walk straight through the Kidron Valley, enter through Jerusalem's eastern gate, and be declared and recognized as KING OF KINGS and LORD OF LORDS. HE will then wage a very brief war with the antichrist and all the nations coming against Israel; HE will defeat and subdue all of them and establish HIS KINGDOM over all of them and the whole Earth for a thousand years. This thousand-year Reign of CHRIST will be a time of complete *peace*, harmony, and prosperity because all evil will have been done away with. And YESHUA will not only be KING OF KINGS for the thousand years but forever.

That is the time we are comparing these SCRIPTURES to, and this is the time that these SCRIPTURES point to. Let's take a look at some of those SCRIPTURES and see what else we can find out about this one-thousand-year long Sabbath.

Both 2 Kings 11:1-12:15 and 2 Chronicles 22:10-24:14 describe the same event. If you read through these chapters carefully, you will find that a 7-year-old son of David is coronated King on the seventh Day while being guarded by *the first* and *the last* divisions of Priests. And immediately afterward, a woman representing both the antichrist and the harlot from Revelation is put to death. she represents the antichrist because she is killing all The King's Sons and GOD'S Covenant People. she also represents the harlot because in her rebellion and disloyalty to GOD, she is trying to establish an order of government that is contrary and unfaithful to the one GOD ordained through the line of David The King. And immediately after she was put to death, there was a time of *peace* during which THE TEMPLE was able to prosper. This event described in Kings and Chronicles is a picture of what will happen immediately after YESHUA'S return.

In 1 Chronicles 28:1-7, THE TEMPLE to be built is called "a house of *rest* for THE ARK OF THE COVENANT." This passage says about David and Solomon that they will both be Kings over Israel forever. Both Kings are pictures of KING YESHUA and what the establishment of HIS KINGDOM will be like because HIS KINGDOM will have no end, and HE will rule and reign forever. HIS KINGDOM will first be established through war with GOD'S help like King David. And then HE will Reign over HIS entire KINGDOM in a time of complete *peace* like King Solomon. This is exactly what we find in 1 Kings 5:3-5 and especially verse 4, which says that THE LORD had given Solomon *rest* on every side. It says in Isaiah 46:9-10 that HE "declares the end from the beginning." These passages we just looked at from Kings and Chronicles are an amazing example of exactly how HE does that. Let's look at one more example like that one.

Whenever THE BIBLE finishes describing one of the days of Creation in Genesis 1:1-31, it follows it up with the phrase, "and there was evening and there was morning the __ day." It says this for every one of the first six days of Creation and by doing so, it also prescribes a beginning and ending for each of those first six days. But when THE BIBLE first mentions the seventh day in Genesis 2:1-3, there is no such prescription for a beginning or an end. There is no mention of evening or morning when it comes to Shabbat, only a Day that is Blessed. An evening or a morning can only be ushered in by the cycle of the sun and the moon. And it is precisely those two things that are deemed unnecessary in both Revelation 21:22-25 and Revelation 22:3-5. In other words, the first Shabbat from Genesis 2:1-3 has no end that is mentioned in the text, and the last Shabbat (which is depicted in the time when THE LORD HIMSELF is ruling and reigning on Earth from The New Jerusalem) literally has no end. And in the same way that the first Shabbat was marked forever as the Day that GOD rested thereby allowing the rest of Creation to also have rest, so too will the Eternal Shabbat begin when THE LORD takes HIS seat on HIS Holy Throne in The New Jerusalem so that HIS People can rest in HIM forever more.

So we can see that when Colossians 2:16-17 calls Shabbat "a shadow of things to come," The Millennial Reign of MESSIAH is one of those "things to come." And so it is the fourth time period that is compared to Shabbat by SCRIPTURE. And The Millennial Reign is not the only time period that fits the description found in Colossians 2:16-17; there is one more mentioned in The Book of Hebrews.

Hebrews 3:7-4:11 is describing a time or state of existence that THE LORD HIMSELF calls "My *Rest*." And the writer makes it very clear that what makes the difference of whether one can enter HIS *Rest* or not is Faith. If you take a close look at 4:4-5 and then 4:9-10, it would be difficult to say that this is not a direct comparison to The Sabbath. But exactly what is this *Rest* that THE LORD is referring to? And in what way is it being compared to Shabbat? There are several verses throughout 4:1-11 that can answer these questions.

Just about the whole context of Hebrews 4:1-11 indicates that the *Rest* being referred to is a future *Rest* that we ourselves can enter into and is not only relevant to the original passage of SCRIPTURE it's quoted from. Verse 8 makes this especially obvious. So because it is referring to a future *Rest* we can enter into, one might think that it could be referring to The Millennial Reign. But verse 10 makes that impossible because we will still be working in The Millennial Reign. So if it's not referring to The Millennial Reign, it could only be referring to one other time. And that time is not within the bounds of time at all. It could only be referring to HEAVEN our Eternal place of *Rest* with THE LORD.

I believe this is another major reason for all the instructions to stop work and rest on Shabbat. Because in HEAVEN we will not have to work to earn our keep, our housing, or our food because our FATHER will provide for us. Isaiah 55:1-3 and Hebrews 4:8-10 together verify this.

In summary, the five different time periods that are directly compared to Shabbat by SCRIPTURE are (1) Creation, (2) Israel's freedom from slavery in Egypt, (3) YESHUA'S Earthly Ministry, (4) The Millennial Kingdom, and (5) HEAVEN Itself. Can you see what else all five of these have in common? Take a moment to think and Pray about it before moving on with the reading and see if THE LORD reveals anything to You. Do You know what it is?

It's THE PRESENCE OF THE LORD. In each of these events and places, THE LORD is physically there among HIS People. And in each one of these, THE PRESENCE OF THE LORD gave them a time of Peace, Rest, and Freedom. So it is safe to say that the true Sabbath Rest is only found in THE PRESENCE OF THE LORD. Now that we've established this, let's revisit the question from the beginning of this study concerning the layout of THE TEMPLE.

First, we discussed what happens at The Altar, what kinds of offerings we ought to bring as gifts to Our LORD on Shabbat and that YESHUA is the only offering that will grant you entry through THE DOOR/VEIL. Next, we highlighted the fact that Shabbat is the time that GOD has set aside for us to enter into HIS PRESENCE and to meet with HIM and that YESHUA HIMSELF is THE DOOR/VEIL by which we can enter into THE PRESENCE OF GOD. But what will it be like when we finally enter through THE DOOR and into HIS PRESENCE? It will be life to us—a place outside of time where we will experience true rest and freedom from the burdensome struggles and concerns of this world. There will be Peace that surpasses all understanding and unspeakable joy. All these things are found only in HIS PRESENCE. And HE has ordained one Day out of every week for us to enter into HIS PRESENCE. The Seventh Day. The Sabbath.

1. Can you see how GOD Teaches us through these similarities and patterns in HIS WORD? If so, how does that make you think of GOD as your Teacher?

_____

_____

_____

2. What would happen if you started reading the whole BIBLE this way?

_____

_____

_____

3. Can you think of any other verses in THE BIBLE that may be pointing to Shabbat or something else in GOD'S plan?

_____

_____

_____

Additional Notes:

_____

_____

_____

_____

_____

_____

CHAPTER 12

Shabbat Remains in The End

Exodus 31:12-17
A Sign and a Covenant forever.

Leviticus 24:1-9
A Sign and a Covenant forever.

Isaiah 56:1-8
THE LORD will not separate the Sabbath
keeping foreigners from HIS People.

Isaiah 58:6-14
THE LORD'S HOLY Day.

Isaiah 60:1-18
The wealth of the nations.

Isaiah 66:15-23
Shabbat is still kept after THE DAY OF THE LORD
and during HIS Reign.

Jeremiah 17:19-27
Kings and Princes who sit on The Throne Of David.

Ezekiel 20:10-26
A Sign and a Covenant forever.

Ezekiel 44:23-24
The Priests in The New TEMPLE will keep HIS Sabbaths Holy.

Matthew 24:15-21
Pray that Your flight from the future great tribulation
will not be on Shabbat.

Matthew 27:57-28:7
Joseph and the two Marys kept Shabbat after YESHUA'S death.

Mark 15:42-16:6
Joseph and the two Marys kept Shabbat after YESHUA'S death.

Luke 23:50-24:6
Joseph and the two Marys kept Shabbat after YESHUA'S death.

John 19:30-20:23
Joseph and the two Marys kept Shabbat after YESHUA'S death.

Acts 16:13
The Apostle Paul kept Shabbat well after YESHUA'S Ascension.

Acts 17:2-4
The Apostle Paul kept Shabbat well after YESHUA'S Ascension.

Acts 18:4-5
The Apostle Paul kept Shabbat well after YESHUA'S Ascension.

Revelation 1:10
John The Revelator still Prayed in THE SPIRIT
on "THE LORD'S Day."

Revelation 20:4-6
They will rule and reign with HIM for a thousand years.

Revelation 21:22-25
The glory of Nations brought as tribute.

Introduction to Chapter 12
Shabbat Is Still Relevant and Still in Effect

So now I have a question for you: Why would Shabbat have gone anywhere? What I mean is this. Considering everything that we've discussed concerning The Sabbath throughout this book and all the goodness that GOD has associated with it, why would anyone teach that it is not for us today? The things that THE SCRIPTURES say about Shabbat not only teach us about THE LORD'S overall prophetic plan for HIS People, but they also teach us about the very character of GOD. So why would anyone think or teach that The Sabbath had been somehow replaced or done away with when SCRIPTURE makes no such claim. In fact, it proves just the opposite in many places. In this last chapter, we will be examining some of those verses.

Exodus 31:12-17
Leviticus 24:1-9
Isaiah 56:1-8
Isaiah 58:6-14
Isaiah 60:1-18
Jeremiah 17:19-27
Ezekiel 20:10-26
Revelation 20:4-6
Revelation 21:22-25

12.1 A Sign and A Covenant Forever

THE LORD HIMSELF says in Ezekiel 20:12 and 20 that The Sabbath is "a sign between me and you." Exodus 31:12-17 says the same thing with a little more detail; verse 13 of this passage also calls The Sabbath "a sign between me and you." But in verses 16-17 THE LORD not only calls Shabbat a sign, but "a sign forever" and "a covenant forever."

In these verses from both Exodus and Ezekiel, these "forever" statements are made about Shabbat itself. But in Leviticus 24:1-9, the same kind of language is used to describe what is to be done every Shabbat. Namely, the arrangement of The Bread of THE PRESENCE. Verse 9 makes it very clear that it is only for The Priests, but verse 8 ends with a very interesting statement about this Bread. HE says, "it is from the people of Israel as a covenant forever."

Needless to say that when THE LORD HIMSELF makes these "forever" statements about Shabbat, "forever" means "forever." But there is something else we can glean from Leviticus 24:8-9. Let's take a look at the details of this "covenant forever." This bread is made from the grain that is brought as a tribute from the rest of The People of Israel to GOD and is only for The Priests to eat. And everyone within sight of The Table of Showbread who was familiar with both Exodus 31:16-17 and Leviticus 24:8-9 would see and be reminded of this "covenant forever" every Shabbat and would begin to associate the "covenant forever" of the Showbread with the "covenant forever" of Shabbat.

It is very similar to the picture that SCRIPTURE gives of what it will be like when The People of GOD will be ruling and reigning with YESHUA for HIS thousand-year reign. A few good reference verses for this would be Isaiah 60:1-18 and Revelation 20:4-6. In this case The Priests would be like GOD'S Chosen Rulers and The People of Israel would be like the nations. That is to say that in the same way the rest of The People of Israel brought tribute to The Priests, so the rest of the nations will bring tribute to those who will be ruling and reigning with CHRIST (Revelation 21:22-25). And in the same way that this Bread is a "covenant forever" from The People of Israel to The Priests, so there will have to be some sort of covenant made from the nations to those who will be ruling and reigning with CHRIST that they would serve them. So the "covenant forever" that The Priests would be reminded of every Sabbath would be a "sign" to them of what would eventually happen during the one-thousand-year long Sabbath.

Maybe you're thinking that's a bit of a stretch. Maybe you're thinking that I'm taking the allegory further than it should go. But before you come to that conclusion, let's take another look at the rewards for keeping Shabbat Holy in Isaiah 56:1-8, Isaiah 58:13-14, and Jeremiah 17:24-26. It may surprise you to find that this concept of tribute being brought from the nations to GOD'S kings actually ties right in with these rewards verses. And if The Sabbath itself is "a covenant forever," then these three passages contain the conditions and promises of that covenant.

1. What comes to your mind when you think of THE LORD calling something a "covenant forever?"

_____

_____

_____

2. Can you think of anything else that THE LORD might have been trying to teach us through The Covenant of The Showbread?

_____

_____

_____

3. The Bread for The Priests was brought from all the other tribes of Israel. What does that tell You about GOD'S Provision for HIS People?

_____

_____

_____

Additional Notes:

_____

_____

_____

_____

_____

_____

_____

Isaiah 58:6-14
Matthew 27:57-28:7
Mark 15:42-16:6
Luke 23:50-24:6
John 19:30-20:23
Acts 16:13
Acts 17:2-4
Acts 18:4-5
Revelation 1:10

12.2 *YESHUA'S Disciples Kept Shabbat*

As we discussed in the previous study, when THE LORD
HIMSELF makes these "forever" statements about Shabbat,
HE really does mean "forever." We have plenty of evidence
from SCRIPTURE that YESHUA'S Disciples kept Shabbat.
And HE had plenty of time to tell HIS Disciples that once HE
was crucified, buried, resurrected, and ascended, they would
no longer need to keep Shabbat and that HE would change it
to sunday. But HE never did. In fact we see just the opposite
happening in SCRIPTURE with multiple occasions when HIS
Disciples are still keeping Shabbat long after The New Covenant
had been established. Let's take a look at some of those examples.

All four of the quoted passages from THE GOSPELS in this study
cover the same event. If you read through these verses carefully,
you will find two things: (1) Joseph of Arimathea made sure that
YESHUA was off The Cross and laid in the tomb before Shabbat
began and (2) The two Marys didn't come back to see the tomb
until after Shabbat was over.

Maybe you're thinking, "Well, they were only late coming back
to the tomb because they were made to wait by someone else."
Maybe you're thinking that legalistic tradition was forced on
them and that's the only reason why they didn't come back until
after Shabbat. Take another look at Luke 23:56; the second half
of this verse says, "On the Sabbath they rested according to the

commandment." It doesn't really get any clearer than that. They rested on Shabbat according to The Commandment of GOD, not the legalistic traditions of men.

And THE GOSPELS are not the only place we find YESHUA'S Disciples keeping Shabbat. In Acts 16:13 both The Apostle Paul and Timothy are seeking a place of Prayer on Shabbat. In Acts 17:2-4 both Paul and Silas are teaching SCRIPTURE and Evangelizing in the Synagogue on Shabbat. And in Acts 18:4-5, Paul is doing the same thing by himself.

And the last example is found in The Book of Revelation. In Revelation 1:10, John says he was "in THE SPIRIT on THE LORD'S Day." Now tradition says that THE LORD'S Day is sunday. It's a good thing for us that YESHUA taught HIS Disciples to stay away from traditions that contradicted THE WORD OF GOD. If you're wondering what day John would have called "THE LORD'S Day," then a quick reference to Isaiah 58:13 will clear it right up for you. In this verse THE LORD HIMSELF refers to The Sabbath as "My Holy Day" and "The Holy Day of THE LORD."

That makes seven Disciples of YESHUA—Joseph of Arimathea, Mary of Magdala, Mary the mother of James, The Apostle Paul, Timothy, Silas, and John The Revelator—who all kept Shabbat in The New Covenant.

1. Has anyone ever told you that keeping The Sabbath was a legalistic tradition?

    _____

    _____

    _____

2. What did they say to you and how did they explain it?

    _____

    _____

    _____

3. What do you think made them come to such a conclusion? Was it THE BIBLE or their own tradition?

    _____

    _____

    _____

Additional Notes:

_____

_____

_____

_____

_____

_____

Isaiah 66:15-23
Ezekiel 44:23-24
Matthew 24:15-21

12.3 Shabbat Remains in The End

In this study we have at least three different prophecies concerning future events during which Shabbat will still be entirely relevant and still in effect. Let's see what they are and what we can find out about them concerning The Sabbath in the end times.

Ezekiel 44:23-24 in context is talking about the roles and responsibilities of The Priesthood that will be serving in the future TEMPLE, which has not even been built yet. And THE LORD says about these Priests in the last part of verse 24, "and they shall keep my Sabbaths Holy."

In Matthew 24:15-21 YESHUA is telling HIS Disciples about the great tribulation that will begin with the antichrist taking over that future TEMPLE. And in verse 20, HE says about that time, "Pray that your flight may not be in winter or on a Sabbath."

Isaiah 66:15-23 is clearly referring to The Day of THE LORD'S Judgment on the nations and afterward during HIS Millennial Reign on Earth. HE says about this time in verse 23, "from Sabbath to Sabbath, all flesh shall come to worship before me."

So why would THE LORD be putting so much emphasis on The Sabbath in these future events if The Sabbath was replaced or done away with? Well . . . HE wouldn't. The fact of the matter is that HE speaks about Shabbat in this way because it never was replaced, it never went anywhere, and it will still be here and being kept by HIS People when HE returns.

1. Has anyone ever told you that The Sabbath was "done away with?" Did they present any SCRIPTURAL evidence?

    _____

    _____

    _____

2. When THE LORD returns, do you want to be found keeping HIS Day Holy or found following the traditions of men?

    _____

    _____

    _____

3. What do you think it will be like in The Millennial Kingdom when everyone will be keeping Shabbat?

    _____

    _____

    _____

Additional Notes:

_____

_____

_____

_____

_____

_____

www.ingramcontent.com/pod-product-compliance
Lightning Source LLC
Chambersburg PA
CBHW071957090426
42740CB00011B/1983